FRENCH PICTURE DICTIONARY COLORING BOOK

Over 1500 French Words and Phrases
for Creative & Visual Learners of All Ages

Color and Learn

Lingo Mastery

ISBN: 978-1-951949-49-5

Free Book Reveals The 6 Step Blueprint That Took Students **From Language Learners To Fluent In 3 Months**

- **6 Unbelievable Hacks** that will accelerate your learning curve

- **Mind Training:** why memorizing vocabulary is easy

- **One Hack To Rule Them All:** This secret nugget will blow you away...

Head over to **LingoMastery.com/hacks** and claim your free book now!

CONTENTS

Introduction 1

Basics of the french Language 2

➞   Adjectives 14

➞   Adverbs 15

➞   Time phrases 15

Les émotions (Emotions) 16

La famille (The Family) 18

Les relations (Relationships) 20

Les valeurs (Values) 22

Le corps humain (The Human Body) 24

À l'intérieur du corps humain (Inside the Human Body) 26

Les animaux domestiques (Pets) 28

Le zoo (The Zoo) 30

Les oiseaux (Birds) 32

QUIZ #1 34

Les reptiles et les amphibiens (Reptiles and Amphibians) 36

Insectes et arachnides (Insects and Arachnids) 38

Les mammifères I (Mammals I) 40

Les mammifères II (Mammals II) 42

Poissons et mollusques (Fish and Mollusks) 44

Les vêtements I (Clothing I) 46

Les vêtements II (Clothing II) 48

La météo (The Weather) 50

Les saisons – Le printemps (The Seasons – Spring) 52

Les saisons – L'été (The Seasons – Summer) 54

QUIZ #2 56

Les saisons – L'automne (The Seasons – Fall/Autumn) 58

Les saisons – L'hiver (The Seasons – Winter) 60

Le temps (Time) 62

La maison (The House) 64

Dans la cuisine (Kitchen Items) 66

Dans la chambre (Bedroom Items) 68

Dans la salle de bains (Bathroom Items) 70

Dans le salon (Living Room Items) 72

Dans la salle à manger (Dining Room Items) 74

QUIZ #3 76

Le jardin (The Garden/The Backyard) 78

La buanderie (The Cleaning Room) 80

L'école / l'université (The School/The University) 82

Le bureau (The Office) 84

Les métiers (Professions/Occupations) 86

Les moyens de transport (Means of Transport) 88

Les paysages (Landscapes) 90

Les sports I (Sports I) 92

Les sports II (Sports II) 94

Noël (Christmas Day) 96

QUIZ #4 98

Instruments de musique (Musical Instruments) 100

Les fruits (Fruits) 102

Les légumes (Vegetables) 104

Les technologies (Technology) 106

Les sciences (Science) 108

L'astronomie (Astronomy) 110

La géographie (Geography) 112

L'hôpital (The Hospital) 114

La ferme (The Farm) 116

QUIZ #5 118

La nourriture (Food) 120

Les plats (Dishes) 122

Les fruits de mer (Seafood) 124

Les formes (Shapes) 126

Le supermarché (The Supermarket) 128

Les médias (Media) 130

Le parc d'attractions (The Fair/The Amusement Park) 132

Les événements importants (Life Events) 134

Les adjectifs I (Adjectives I) 136

QUIZ #6 138

Les adjectifs II (Adjectives II) 140

Les adverbes (Adverbs) 142

Les directions (Directions) 144

Le restaurant (The Restaurant) 146

Le centre commercial (The Mall) 148

Les verbes I (Verbs I) 150

Les verbes II (Verbs II) 152

Construction I (Construction I) 154

Construction II (Construction II) 156

QUIZ #7 158

Les plantes et arbres (Plants and Trees) 160

Le carnaval (The Carnival) 162

L'atelier (The Workshop) 164

L'épicerie (The Grocery Store) 166

Voyage I (Travel and Living I) 168

Voyage II (Travel and Living II) 170

Les jouets (Toys) 172

La fête d'anniversaire (The Birthday Party) 174

Les opposés (Opposites) 176

QUIZ #8 178

Conclusion 180

Answers 181

INTRODUCTION

This French Picture Dictionary Coloring Book is a fun vocabulary building tool with illustrations that you can color while studying. It covers an immense range of topics that will help you learn everything related to the French language in daily subjects, from members of the family and animals to parts of the body and describing jobs.

This introduction is a guide to help you get started in French and polish your basic grammar, spelling, punctuation, and vocabulary skills. Good luck – and **most importantly, enjoy yourself!**

BASICS OF THE FRENCH LANGUAGE

I.   Spelling and Pronunciation

a. The French Alphabet – a Built-in Guide to Pronunciation.

There are certain letters that you pronounce differently in your native language and in French. Some letters may not even exist in your language. You must therefore learn to recognize these letters and to pronounce them correctly.

A (*ah*)	H (*ahsh*)	O (*oh*)	V (*vay*)
B (*bay*)	I (*ee*)	P (*pay*)	W (*doobl-vay*)
C (*say*)	J (*zhee*)	Q (*kü*)	X (*eeks*)
D (*day*)	K (*kah*)	R (*airr*)	Y (*ee-grek*)
E (*er*)	L (*el*)	S (*ess*)	Z (*zed*)
F (*ef*)	M (*em*)	T (*tay*)	
G (*zhay*)	N (*en*)	U (*ü*)	

To improve your pronunciation, you must also learn to pronounce letter combinations such as "*eau*", "*ueil*", "*gn*", "*en*"...

b. Pronunciation

The best way to acquire a good French pronunciation is to listen, as often as you can, to movies, or radio broadcasts. You will notice that French contains several nasal sounds that are not used in English, which can only be learned by listening and imitating. Here is a quick guide of how to pronounce the most common letter combinations:

Vowels

A -> sounds like *ah* -> as in *hat*

E/EU -> sounds like *euh* -> as in *fur*

É -> sounds like *hey* -> as in *café*

È/Ê -> sounds like *hay* -> as in *air*

I/Y -> sounds like *ee* -> as in *pit*

O/AU/EAU -> sounds like *oh* -> as in *paw/gâteau*

OI -> sounds like *wah* -> as in *swan*

U -> sounds like *u* -> as in *tutu, übermensch*

OU -> sounds like *oo* -> as in *fool*

Consonants

C + E/I/Ç -> sounds like *ss* -> as in *center, ici, ça va?, Celia*

C + other letters -> sounds like *kah* -> as in *Canada, combien*

CH -> sounds like *sh* -> as in *chambre, shell*

G + E/I -> sounds like *je* -> as in *étage, garage*

G + other letters -> sounds like *geh* -> as in *garage, grammar*

GN -> sounds like *nyeh* -> as in *champagne, piña colada*

H -> is *silent!* -> as in *j'habite, heir*

QU -> sounds like *keh* -> as in *question, quiche*

LL -> sounds like *elle* -> as in *shell, ville*

LL -> sounds like *yeh* -> as in *fille, je travaille*

A few more rules

- In French, you pronounce **j, b, d, p, t** more softly than in English, while the letter **r** is rolled a lot more.
- Usually in French, the last consonant of a word is not sounded (chat = *cha*, chaud = *cho*)
- When a word ends in an s and is followed by a vowel, you can link both sounds together. This is called a *liaison:* Vous êtes français = Vouz**z**êtes français.

Grammar – Verbs and Tenses

I-   Glossary

Verb: A doing word. It describes an <u>action.</u>

Tense: It tells you <u>when</u> an action happens/happened/will happen, etc…

Subject: It refers to <u>who</u> is doing the action. There will be a different ending for each person.

singular	je	*I*
	tu	*you (informal)*
	il/elle	*he/she*
plural	nous	*we*
	vous	*you (formal and group)*
	ils/elles	*they*

Ending: Usually the last two letters in a word, it will tell you what tense you are in and what person you are using.

Stem/Root: It's what is left of the verb once the ending is gone OR it is the part you will be using from the infinitive form.

Infinitive: The only form of the verb you will find in the dictionary. It usually ends in ER, IR or RE.

Regular verbs: A verb that always follows standard patterns.

Irregular verbs: A verb that will EITHER not follow a pattern OR will have an irregular root.

Auxiliary verbs: In French, there are 2 auxiliary verbs: AVOIR and ETRE.

AVOIR	*TO HAVE*
J'ai	*I have*
Tu as	*You (singular) have*
Il / Elle a	*He / She has*
Nous avons	*We have*

Vous avez	*You (plural) have*
Ils / Elles ont	*They have*
ÊTRE	**TO BE**
Je suis	*I am*
Tu es	*You (singular) are*
Il / Elle est	*He / She is*
Nous sommes	*We are*
Vous êtes	*You (plural) are*
Ils / Elles sont	*They are*

II-   The Present Tense

It tells you what happens as a general rule or what is happening.

a) How to build it

Remove the ending from the infinitive which can be either ER, IR, RE. Then, add the following endings instead:

	ER	**IR**	**RE**
je	*-e*	*-is*	*-s*
tu	*-es*	*-is*	*-s*
il	*-e*	*-it*	
nous	*-ons*	*-issons*	*-ons*
vous	*-ez*	*-issez*	*-ez*
ils	*-ent*	*-issent*	*-ent*

Ex: Accepter (to accept) *-> Accept -> Tu acceptes* (you accept)

Finir (to finish) *-> Fini -> Nous finissons* (we finish)

Vendre (to sell) *-> Vend -> Je vends* (I sell)

ATTENTION:

- Acheter (to buy): for je, tu, il, elle, on, ils, elles the root becomes *achèt_*
- Appeler (to call): for je, tu, il, elle, on, ils, elles the root becomes *appell_*
- Jeter (to throw): for je, tu, il, elle, on, ils, elles the root becomes *jett_*
- Espérer (to hope): for je, tu, il, elle, on, ils, elles the root becomes *espèr_*
- Employer (to employ): for je, tu, il, elle, on, ils, elles the root becomes *emploi_*
- Also note that verbs ending in *–ger* will be spelt *-geons* in the nous form and verbs ending in *–cer* will be spelt *-çons* in the nous form.

b) Uses of the present tense

- To say what happens repeatedly (every year, every day, on Tuesdays).
- To say what is happening at the present time.
- To say what is happening in the immediate future.
- To say what has been happening for a period of time or since a particular time and is still happening.

III-   The Future Tense

It tells you what will happen.

a) How to build it

This time you will add the following endings to the full infinitive (without getting rid of *-ER* and *-RE* first, *-RE* verbs drop the E only).

je	*-ai*
tu	*-as*
il / elle / on	*-a*
nous	*-ons*
vous	*-ez*
ils / elles	*-ont*

Ex: *Manger* (to eat) -> *je mangerai* (I will eat)

ATTENTION:

Some verbs do not follow the previous rule. Instead of using the full infinitive, you must use these stems instead:

- Aller (to go) becomes *ir-*
- Envoyer (to send) becomes *enverr-*
- Courir (to run) becomes *courr-*
- Mourir (to die) becomes *mourr-*
- Tenir (to hold) becomes *tiendr-*
- Venir (to come) becomes *viendr-*
- Etre (to be) becomes *ser-*
- Faire (to do) becomes *fer-*
- S'asseoir (to sit) becomes *s'assiér-*
- Avoir (to have) becomes *aur-*
- Devoir (to have to) becomes *devr-*
- Pleuvoir (to rain) becomes *pleuvr-*
- Pouvoir (to be able to) becomes *pour-*
- Recevoir (to receive) becomes *recevr-*
- Savoir (to know) becomes *saur-*
- Voir (to see) becomes *verr-*

Also: see section in present tense, as the same spelling change will happen in the future tense.

b) Uses of the future tense

- To say what will happen.
- You will have to use the future tense after time expressions such as *quand* and *aussitôt que.*

IV-   The Conditional Tense

It tells you what would/may/might happen.

a) How to build it

Like you did with the future tense, you will add the following endings to the full infinitive.

je	-ais
tu	-ais
il / elle / on	-ait
nous	-ions
vous	-iez
ils / elles	-aient

ATTENTION:

The same exceptions as the future tense apply.

b) Uses of the conditional tense

- To say what would happen.
- Often used as a combination with si + imperfect tense to express a condition.
- To soften requests or commands (could you...?).
- Used in reported speech.

V- The Imperfect Tense

It is used to describe what used to happen or what was going on at some point in the past.

a) How to build it

Remove the ER, IR, RE from the infinitive and add the following endings:

	ER	IR	RE
je	-ais	-issais	-ais
tu	-ais	-issais	-ais
il	-ait	-issait	-ait
nous	-ions	-issions	-ions
vous	-iez	-issiez	-iez
ils	-aient	-issaient	-aient

ATTENTION:

Again, note that some roots are irregular:

- Boire (to drink) becomes *buv-*
- Dire (to say) becomes *dis-*
- Ecrire (to write) becomes *écriv-*
- Conduire (to drive) becomes *conduis-*
- Devoir (to have to) becomes *dev-*
- Faire (to do) becomes *fais-*
- Falloir (to have to) becomes *fall-*
- Lire (to read) becomes *lis-*
- Pleuvoir (to rain) becomes *pleuv-*
- Prendre (to take) becomes *pren-*
- Recevoir (to receive) becomes *recev-*
- Savoir (to know) becomes *sav-*
- Voir (to see) becomes *voy-*
- Vouloir (to want) becomes *voul-*

b) Uses of the imperfect

- To say what was happening.
- To say what you were doing in the past.
- To say what used to happen.
- To describe how a situation was in the past.

VI- The Past Tense with AVOIR

It tells you what has happened, what you have done in the past, or what happened.

a) How to build it

It is a compound (composé) tense. It consists of two words: the auxiliary verb and the past participle. The auxiliary is usually AVOIR.

1- Regular verbs

The past participle and perfect tense of these verbs are formed as follows: remove the ending off the infinitive and add the following endings instead.

	ER	IR	RE
j'ai	-é	-i	-u
tu as	-é	-i	-u
il a	-é	-i	-u
nous avons	-é	-i	-u
vous avez	-é	-i	-u
ils ont	-é	-i	-u
ex:	j'ai regardé	j'ai fini	j'ai vendu

<u>Ex:</u> *Manger* (to eat) -> *Mang* -> *Mangé* -> *J'ai mangé* (I ate)

2- Irregular verbs

Here is a list of the main irregular past participles:

apprendre	*appris*
avoir	*eu*
boire	*bu*
conduire	*conduit*
connaître	*connu*
coudre	*cousu*
courir	*couru*
couvrir	*couvert*

falloir	*fallu*
lire	*lu*
mettre	*mis*
ouvrir	*ouvert*
peindre	*peint*
pleuvoir	*plu*
pouvoir	*pu*
prendre	*pris*

croire	*cru*
découvrir	*découvert*
devoir	*dû*
dire	*dit*
écrire	*écrit*
éteindre	*éteint*
être	*été*
faire	*fait*

promettre	*promis*
recevoir	*reçu*
rire	*ri*
savoir	*su*
sourire	*souri*
traduire	*traduit*
voir	*vu*
vouloir	*voulu*

3- Making the perfect tense negative

You will wrap the ne/n' ... pas around the auxiliary.

Ex: *J'ai mangé* (I ate) -> *Je n'ai pas mangé* (I did not eat)

4- Uses of the perfect tense

- To say what has happened.
- To say what you have done.
- To say what happened or what you did.

VII- The Past tense with ÊTRE

It will be used in the same way as the *avoir* verbs but... you have to make the past participle agree with the person or thing that is doing the action (like adjectives). There is a precise list of verbs that use *être* instead of *avoir*:

M	MONTER	*monté*
R	RESTER	*resté*
S	SORTIR	*sorti*

11

V	VENIR	*venu*
A	ARRIVER	*arrive*
N	NAITRE	*né*
D	DESCENDRE	*descendu*
E	ENTRER	*entré*
T	TOMBER	*tombé*
R	RENTRER	*rentré*
A	ALLER	*allé*
M	MOURIR	*mort*
P	PARTIR	*parti*

Instead of using *avoir* in the present tense as the auxiliary, you will need to use the conjugated *être*.

ÊTRE
Je suis
Tu es
Il / Elle / On est
Nous sommes
Vous êtes
Ils / Elles sont

Ex: *Je suis allé* (I went) / *Elle est sortie* (She went out) / *Il est parti* (He left) / *Elles sont devenues* (They have become).

1- Agreement rules

➔ When using **être** as the auxiliary, add **-e to the past participle** if the subject is feminine.

Entrer → Elle est entrée.

➔ When using **être** as the auxiliary, add -**s to the past participle** if the subject is masculine plural (or includes masculine **and** feminine).

Arriver → *Ils sont arrivés.*

➔ When using **être** as the auxiliary, add –**es to the past participle** if the subject is feminine plural.

Partir → *Elles sont parties.*

Adjectives: when using adjectives in French, it is essential that the ending of the adjective matches the gender of the nouns that it refers to. Nouns are either feminine or masculine. You may need to look a word up in the dictionary to find out if it is feminine or masculine. Otherwise, check the articles that are used in front of the noun. If it says 'une' or 'la' (one/the) then the noun is feminine (*la table, une chaise*). If it says 'un' or 'le', then the noun is masculine (*un canapé, le chien*). Finally, if the noun has the word 'les' or 'des' (the/some) in front of it, it is plural (*des voitures, les lampes*), regardless of whether it is masculine or feminine.

So how do adjectives change according to the gender of the noun? This table will summarize it all:

Kind of adjective	Masc.singular	Fem.singular	Masc.plural	Fem.plural
Most adjectives, e.g *grand*	Don't add anything	Add 'e'	Add 's'	Add 'es'
Ending in 'e'	Don't add anything	Don't add anything	Add 's'	Add 's'
Ending in 's'	Don't add anything	Add 'e'	Don't add anything	Add 'es'
Ending in 'eux'	Don't add anything	Change 'x' to 'se'	Don't add anything	Change 'x' to 'ses'
Ending in 'f'	Don't add anything	Change 'f' to 've'	Add 's'	Change 'f' to 'ves'

Ex: grand (tall – masculine) -> *grande* (tall – feminine) -> *grandes* (tall – feminine plural)

Heureux (happy – masculine) -> *heureuse* (happy – feminine) -> *heureux* (happy – masculine plural).

Actif (active – masculine) -> *active* (active – feminine) -> *actives* (active – faminine plural).

Some adjectives do not follow these rules so you need to memorize them:

Masc.sing	Fem.sing	Masc.plural	Fem.plural	English
Bon	Bonne	Bons	Bonnes	*Good*
Beau	Belle	Beaux	Belles	*Beautiful*
Nouveau	Nouvelle	Nouveaux	Nouvelles	*New*
Vieux	Vieille	Vieux	Vieilles	*Old*
Blanc	Blanche	Blancs	Blanches	*White*
Long	Longue	Longs	Longues	*Long*
Gros	Grosse	Gros	Grosses	*Big*
Fou	Folle	Fous	Folles	*Crazy*

VIII- Word Order

Key rules:

➢ Adjectives

✓ Normally go **AFTER** their **nouns**

Je	dors	sur	un	lit	confortable
I	*sleep*	*on*	*a*	*bed*	*comfortable*

✓ Some very **short frequent adjectives** go **BEFORE their nouns**:

Je	dors	sur	un	grand	lit.
I	*sleep*	*on*	*a*	*big*	*bed*

Learn them by heart; it's easier to split them into three groups of related adjectives :

grand – gros – petit;   jeune – vieux – ancien ; beau (belle) – joli

➢ Adverbs

✓ If they **describe the verb,** they tend to go **straight after it**: *Je chante **bien*** = *I sing **well***. We rarely split subject and verbs in French and never for adverbs.
✓ If they **describe an adjective,** they tend to go **just before it**: *C'est une **très** vieille maison* = *It's a **very** old house.*

➢ Time phrases

✓ **They are found either** at the start or at the end **of the sentence** if **they are made up of** several words **(e.g.** *le weekend dernier* (last weekend)*, tous les jours* (everyday)*,* **etc).**
✓ Single word **time phrases** (*toujours* (always)*, normalement* (usually)*, souvent* (often)) **can go** straight after **the** verb or at the end **of the sentences.**

➔ **Never place a time phrase between the subject and the verb in French.**

~~Je souvent mange de la pizza~~ *(I often eat pizza)*.

Instead, say: Je mange souvent de la pizza *or* Souvent, je mange de la pizza.

LES ÉMOTIONS (EMOTIONS)

1) **heureux** (happy)
heu-RREH

2) **triste** (sad)
tree-STEH

3) **excité** (excited)
ex-see-TEY

4) **en colère** (angry)
an-coh-leh-RE

5) **surpris** (surprised)
sur-PREE

6) **soucieux** (concerned)
soo-see-YEUH

7) **effrayé** (scared)
eff-ray-YAY

8) **curieux** (curious)
queue-ree-YEH

9) **diverti** (amused)
dee-ver-TEE

10) **confus** (confused)
con-FU

11) **malade** (sick)
mah-lah-DE

12) **coquin** (naughty)
coh-KIN

13) **sérieux** (serious)
se-ree-YEH

14) **concentré** (focused)
con-cent-RAY

15) **ennuyé** (bored)
an-nwee-YEH

16) **dépassé** (overwhelmed)
day-pass-HEY

17) **amoureux** (in love)
ah-moo-REUH

18) **honteux** (ashamed)
hon-TEUH

19) **anxieux** (anxious)
ankss-YEUH

20) **dégoûté** (disgusted)
day-goo-teyTEY

21) **offensé** (offended)
oh-fan-SAY

22) **souffrant** (sore)
soo-FRAN

Il est en colère contre toi.
He is angry at you.

Mes grands-parents sont toujours aussi amoureux.
My grandparents are still very much in love.

Le repas d'hier m'a rendu malade.
Yesterday's meal made me sick.

LA FAMILLE (THE FAMILY)

1) **grands-parents** (grandparents)
gran-pah-RANT

2) **grand-mère** (grandmother)
gran-may-REH

3) **grand-père** (grandfather)
gran-pay-REH

4) **oncle** (uncle)
on-k-LEH

5) **mère** (mother)
may-REH

6) **père** (father)
pay-REH

7) **tante** (aunt)
tan-TEH

8) **cousin** (cousin, m.)
coo-z-UN

9) **frère** (brother)
frey-REH

10) **moi** (me)
MWAH

11) **mari / femme** (husband/wife)
mah-REE

12) **sœur** (sister)
ss-HEUR

13) **cousine** (cousin, f.)
coo-zee-NEH

14) **neveu** (nephew)
neh-VEH

15) **fils** (son)
fee-SS

16) **fille** (daughter)
fee-YEH

17) **nièce** (niece)
nee-YES

18) **petit-fils** (grandson)
peh-tee-fee-SS

19) **petite-fille** (granddaughter)
peh-tee-the-fee-YEH

20) **cousin éloigné** (second cousin)
coo-z-un-hey-lwah-GNEY

- **Belle famille (In-laws)**
– Proches (Relatives)

bel-fah-me-YEH

– pro-CH

21) **beau-père** (father-in-law)
beau-pay-REH

22) **belle-mère** (mother-in-law)
belle-may-REH

23) **beau-frère** (brother-in-law)
beau-frey-REH

24) **belle-sœur** (sister-in-law)
bell-ss-HEUR

25) **belle-fille** (daughter-in-law)
belle-fee-YEH

26) **beau-fils** (son-in-law)
beau-fee-SS

27) **oncle par alliance** (uncle-in-law)
on-k-leh-parr-ah-lee-YANCE

28) **tante par alliance** (aunt-in-law)
tan-the-parr-ah-lee-YANCE

Tu es bien la fille de ton père !
You really are your father's daughter!

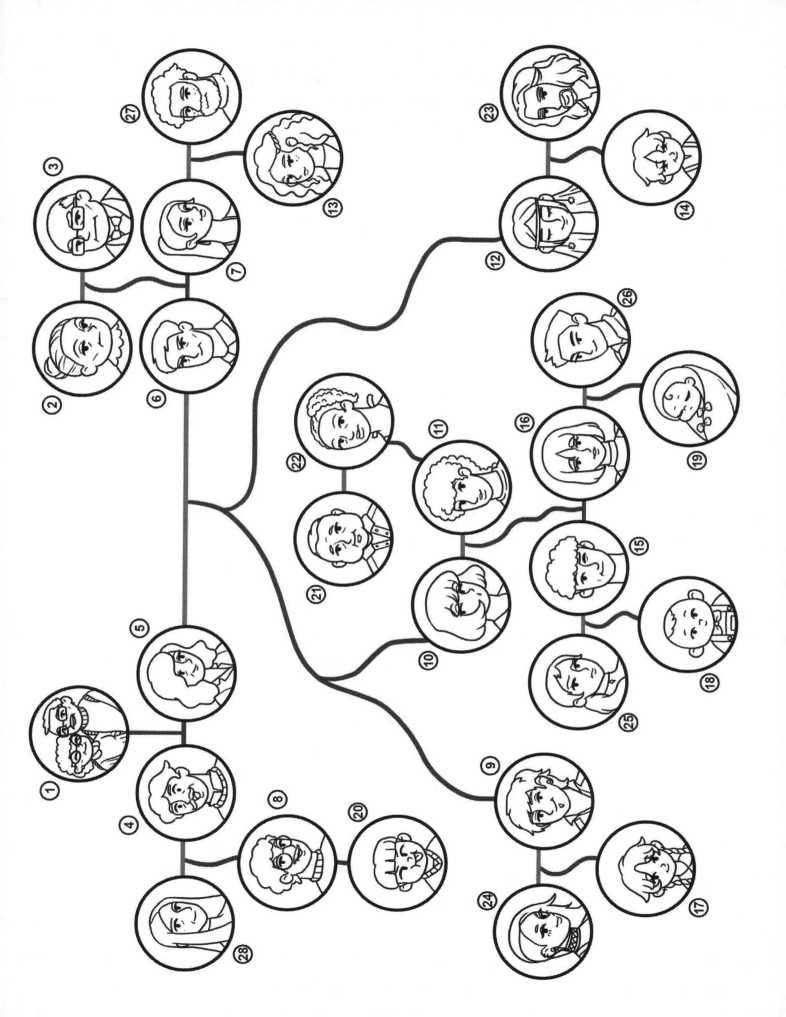

LES RELATIONS (RELATIONSHIPS)

1) **couple marié** (married couple)
coo-pleh-mah-ree-YAY

2) **homme marié** (married man)
ome-mah-ree-YAY

3) **femme mariée** (married woman)
fah-meh-mah-ree-YAY

4) **couple divorcé** (divorced couple)
coo-pleh-dee-vor-SAY

5) **ex-femme** (ex-wife)
ex-fah-MEH

6) **ex-mari** (ex-husband)
ex-mah-REE

7) **ami** (friend)
ah-MEE

8) **petite-amie** (girlfriend)
peh-titeh-ah-MEE

9) **petit-ami** (boyfriend)
peh-tit-ah-MEE

10) **voisin** (neighbor)
vwah-ZIN

11) **célibataire** (single)
say-lee-bah-tay-REH

12) **divorcé(e)** (divorcée/divorcé)
dee-vor-SAY

13) **veuf** (widower)
v-HEUF

14) **veuve** (widow)
veu-VEH

Pauline a un nouveau petit-ami.
Pauline has a new boyfriend.

Je suis célibataire depuis l'année dernière.
I have been single since last year.

Ma voisine est très curieuse.
My neighbor is very curious.

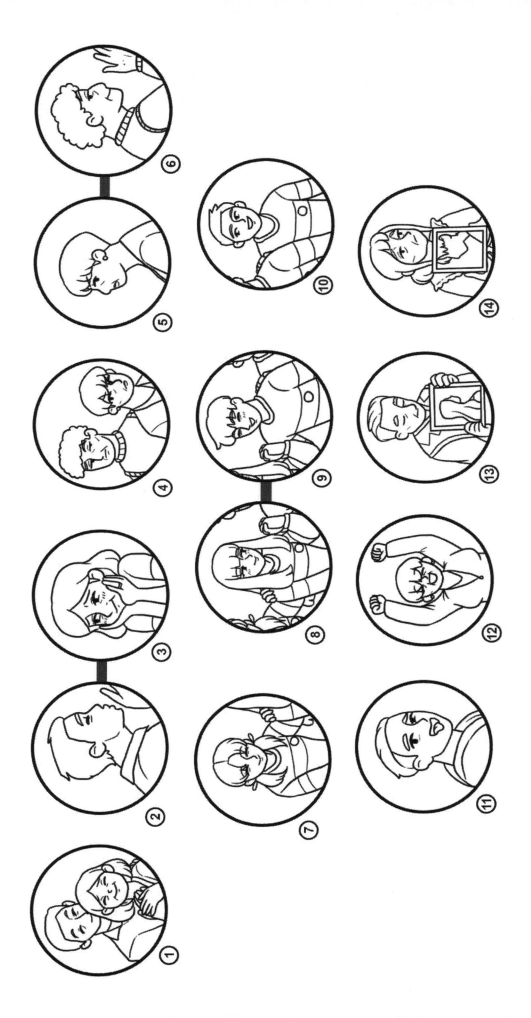

LES VALEURS (VALUES)

1) **respect** (respect)
ress-PEY

2) **gratitude** (gratitude)
grah-tee-tu-DEH

3) **tolérance** (tolerance)
toh-ley-ran-CEH

4) **collaboration** (collaboration)
co-lah-bo-rah-see-YON

5) **honnêteté** (honesty)
O-net-TAY

6) **tempérance** (temperance)
ten-pay-ran-CEH

7) **responsabilité** (responsibility)
ress-pon-sah-bee-lee-TAY

8) **foi** (faith)
FWAH

9) **courage** (courage)
coo-rah-GE

10) **gentillesse** (kindness)
gen-tee-YES

11) **engagement** (commitment)
an-gah-geh-MAN

12) **enthousiasme** (enthusiasm)
an-too-ziah-SME

13) **confiance** (trust)
con-fee-yan-CEH

14) **ponctualité** (punctuality)
ponk-tuh-ah-lee-TAY

L'honnêteté est très importante dans un couple.
Honesty is very important in a couple.

J'ai confiance en toi.
I trust you.

J'ai beaucoup de responsabilités au travail.
I have a lot of responsibilities at work.

LE CORPS HUMAIN (THE HUMAN BODY)

1) **tête** (head)
   tey-TEH

2) **cheveux** (hair)
   cheh-VEU

3) **visage** (face)
   vee-sah-GE

4) **front** (forehead)
   f-RON

5) **oreille** (ear)
   oh-ray-YEH

6) **yeux** (eyes)
   zee-YEUH

7) **nez** (nose)
   NEY

8) **joue** (cheek)
   JOO

9) **bouche** (mouth)
   boo-CHEH

10) **menton** (chin)
    man-TON

11) **cou** (neck)
    COO

12) **dos** (back)
    DOH

13) **poitrine** (chest)
    pwa-tree-NEH

14) **épaule** (shoulder)
    hey-poh-LEH

15) **bras** (arm)
    BRA

16) **avant-bras** (forearm)
    ah-van-BRA

17) **main** (hand)
    m-UN

18) **ventre** (abdomen)
    van-TREH

19) **taille** (waist)
    tah-YEH

20) **hanche** (hip)
    an-CH

21) **jambe** (leg)
    jam-BEH

22) **cuisse** (thigh)
    cuee-SS

23) **genou** (knee)
    geh-NOO

24) **mollet** (calf)
    moh-LEY

25) **tibia** (shin)
    tee-bee-YAH

26) **pied** (foot)
    pee-YAY

Je me suis cassé le bras quand j'avais 7 ans.
I broke my arm when I was 7.

Tu as encore mal au dos?
Does your back still hurt?

Il m'a donné un coup de pied dans la jambe.
He kicked me in the leg.

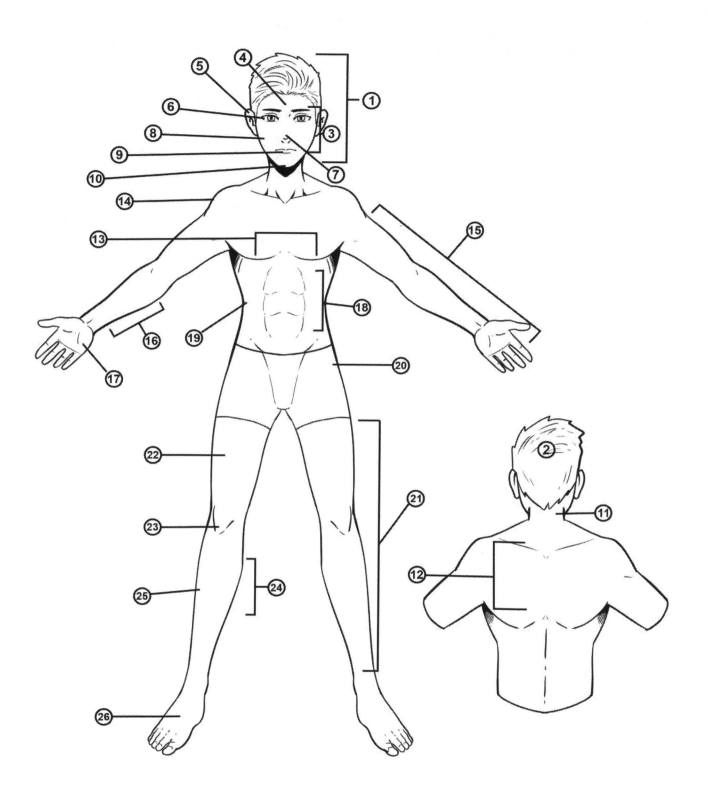

À L'INTÉRIEUR DU CORPS HUMAIN (INSIDE THE HUMAN BODY)

1) **peau** (skin)
POH

2) **muscles** (muscles)
mu-ss-CLEH

3) **os** (bones)
oh-SS

4) **cerveau** (brain)
ser-VOH

5) **thyroïde** (thyroid)
tee-roh-ee-DEH

6) **veines** (veins)
vay-NEH

7) **artères** (arteries)
arr-tay-REH

8) **cœur** (heart)
KEUR

9) **poumons** (lungs)
poo-MON

10) **estomac** (stomach)
ess-toh-MAH

11) **œsophage** (esophagus)
euh-zo-fa-GEH

12) **pancréas** (pancreas)
pan-cray-ASS

13) **foie** (liver)
FWAH

14) **petit intestin** (small intestine)
peh-tee-in-test-UN

15) **gros intestin** (large intestine)
groh-in-test-UN

16) **vésicule biliaire** (gallbladder)
vey-zee-cule-bee-lee-HAIR

17) **reins** (kidneys)
rr-UN

18) **vessie** (urinary bladder)
vay-SEE

J'ai eu une opération des reins.
I had an operation on my kidneys.

Fumer est mauvais pour les poumons.
Smoking is bad for the lungs.

J'ai des brûlures d'estomac.
I have heartburn.

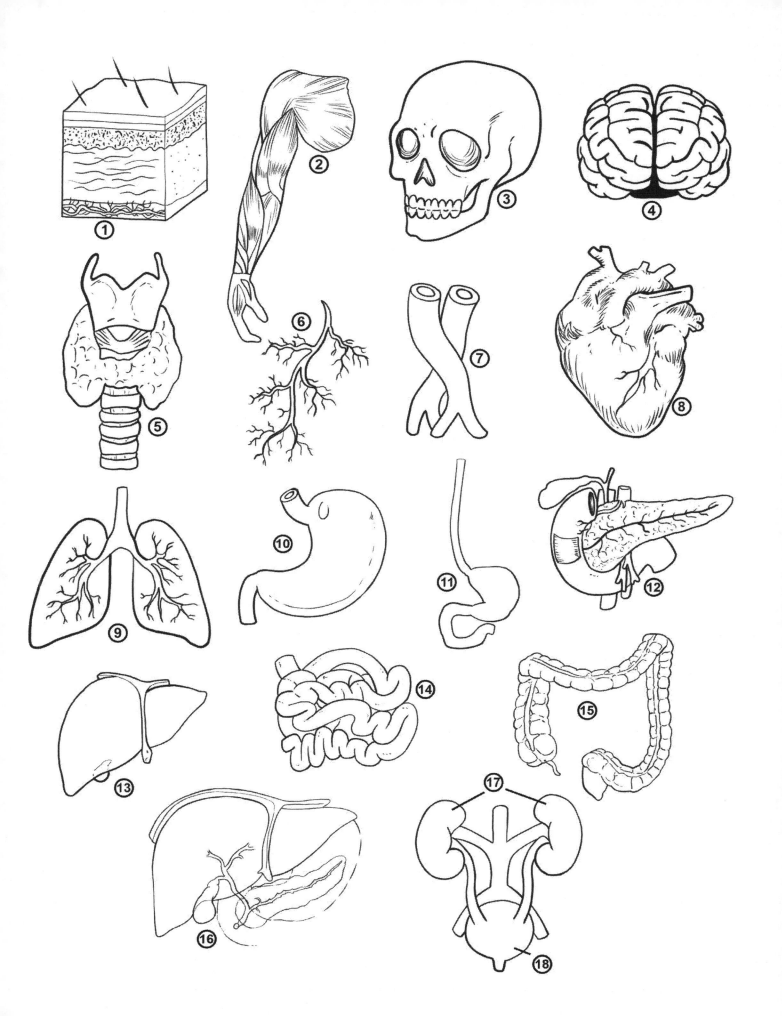

LES ANIMAUX DOMESTIQUES (PETS)

1) **chien** (dog)
   chee-YUN

2) **chat** (cat)
   CHAH

3) **furret** (ferret)
   fu-RAY

4) **cochon nain** (mini pig/teacup pig)
   coh-chon-NUN

5) **cheval** (horse)
   che-vah-LEH

6) **scalaire** (angelfish)
   ska-lay-REH

7) **poisson clown** (clown fish)
   pwah-ss-on-CLOWN

8) **poisson rouge** (goldfish)
   pwah-ss-on-roo-GEH

9) **hamster** (hamster)
   hams-TER

10) **cochon d'inde** (guinea pig)
    coh-chon-d-un-DEH

11) **souris** (mouse)
    soo-REE

12) **lapin** (rabbit)
    lah-PIN

13) **hérisson** (hedgehog)
    hey-ree-ss-ON

14) **tarentule** (tarantula)
    tah-ren-TULE

15) **colonie de fourmis** (ant colony)
    coh-loh-nee-deh-foor-ME

16) **tortue** (tortoise)
    tor-TUH

17) **serpent** (snake)
    say-r-PAN

18) **caméléon** (chameleon)
    cah-may-lay-ON

19) **iguane** (iguana)
    ee-GUAHN

20) **canari** (canary)
    cah-nah-REE

21) **perroquet** (parrot)
    pay-roh-KAY

22) **perruche** (parakeet)
    pay-ru-CHEH

Je préfère les chiens aux chats.
I prefer dogs over cats.

J'ai offert un poisson rouge à ma fille.
I gifted a goldfish to my daughter.

Il faut sauver les tortues.
We must save tortoises.

LE ZOO (THE ZOO)

1) **éléphant** (elephant)
   hey-ley-FAN

2) **rhinocéros** (rhino)
   ree-noh-say-ROS

3) **girafe** (giraffe)
   gee-rah-FEH

4) **zèbre** (zebra)
   zay-BREH

5) **hippopotame** (hippopotamus)
   hee-poh-poh-TAM

6) **guépard** (cheetah)
   gay-PAR

7) **tigre** (tiger)
   tee-GREH

8) **lion** (lion)
   lee-YON

9) **chimpanzé** (chimpanzee)
   ch-un-panz-HEY

10) **orang-outan** (orangutan)
    oh-ran-oo-TAN

11) **babouin** (baboon)
    bah-boo-WUN

12) **kangourou** (kangaroo)
    kan-goo-ROO

13) **koala** (koala)
    koh-ah-LAH

14) **lémurien** (lemur)
    lay-mu-ree-YEN

Le lion est le roi des animaux.
The lion is the king of animals.

J'ai caressé un koala en Australie.
I petted a koala in Australia.

Les éléphants sont très intelligents.
Elephants are very intelligent.

LES OISEAUX (BIRDS)

1) **autruche** (ostrich)
oh-tru-SH

2) **paon** (peacock)
PAN

3) **dinde** (turkey)
dun-DEH

4) **coq** (rooster)
COK

5) **canard** (duck)
cah-NAR

6) **cygne** (swan)
see-GNEH

7) **pélican** (pelican)
pay-lee-CAN

8) **flamant rose** (flamingo)
flah-man-ROHZ

9) **pigeon** (pigeon)
pee-JON

10) **chouette** (owl)
choo-WETTE

11) **vautour** (vulture)
voh-TOUR

12) **aigle** (eagle)
hay-GLEH

13) **mouette** (seagull)
moo-ETTE

14) **corbeau** (crow)
kor-BEAU

15) **toucan** (toucan)
too-CAN

16) **pingouin** (penguin)
pin-goo-UN

17) **pic** (woodpecker)
PIK

18) **ara** (macaw)
ARAH

19) **colibri** (hummingbird)
coh-lee-BREE

20) **kiwi** (kiwi)
kee-WEE

Le coq est le symbole de la France.
The rooster is the symbol of France.

Il est fier comme un paon.
He is proud as a peacock.

Nous allons manger de la dinde pour Noël.
We are going to eat turkey for Christmas.

QUIZ #1

Use arrows to match the corresponding translations:

a. goldfish	1. triste
b. leg	2. petit fils
c. brother	3. nez
d. serious	4. cerveau
e. flamingo	5. gentillesse
f. mouse	6. guépard
g. cheetah	7. curieux
h. neighbor	8. chat
i. cat	9. flamant rose
j. sad	10. frère
k. kindness	11. jambe
l. grandson	12. souris
m. girlfriend	13. poisson rouge
n. curious	14. voisin
o. brain	15. sérieux
p. nose	16. petit-amie

Fill in the blank spaces with the options below (use each word only once):

Ma _____ et mon père ne sont plus ensemble depuis des années. Tout le monde est toujours _____ de voir à quel point ils s'entendent bien pour un _____. Ma _____ est ma meilleure amie. Elle est d'une grande _____ et elle a un _____ d'or. Quant à moi, je suis _____ et tout le monde dit que j'ai beaucoup de _____. J'adore les animaux, surtout les _____. Demain soir, nous sommes invités chez mon père pour dîner. Je crois qu'il va préparer une _____. J'espère que je me sentirai mieux d'ici là car aujourd'hui, j'ai très mal à la _____ et j'ai le nez _____.

surpris   gentillesse

courage   sœur

dinde   chiens

couple divorcé   bouché

cœur   tête

mère   sérieux

LES REPTILES ET LES AMPHIBIENS (REPTILES AND AMPHIBIANS)

- **Reptiles (Reptiles)**
  rep-tee-LEH

1) **anaconda** (anaconda)
   ah-nah-con-DAH

2) **cobra royal** (king cobra)
   koh-bra-roh-YAL

3) **crotale** (rattlesnake)
   croh-tah-LEH

4) **serpent de corail** (coral snake)
   ser-pan-deuh-coh-RAIL

5) **lézard à cornes** (horned lizard)
   lay-zar-ah-KORN

6) **lézard à collerette** (frill-necked lizard)
   lay-zar-ah-col-ray-TEH

7) **lézard Jésus-Christ** (common basilisk/Jesus Christ lizard)
   lay-zar-jay-zu-KREE

8) **dragon de Komodo** (Komodo dragon)
   grah-gon-deuh-KOMODO

9) **crocodile** (crocodile)
   kro-ko-dee-LEH

10) **gavial du Gange** (gharial/gavial)
    gah-vee-yal-duh-GANGE

11) **tortue de mer** (sea turtle)
    tor-tue-deuh-MER

- **Amphibiens (Amphibians)**
  an-fee-bee-YEEN

12) **salamandre** (salamander)
    sah-lah-man-DREH

13) **grenouille goliath** (Goliath frog)
    gre-noo-ye-gohlee-AT

Cette rivière est pleine de crocodiles.
This river is full of crocodiles.

J'ai un dragon de Komodo dans mon vivarium.
I have a Komodo dragon in my vivarium.

Il faut protéger les tortues de mer de la pollution.
We must protect sea turtles from pollution.

INSECTES ET ARACHNIDES (INSECTS AND ARACHNIDS)

- **Insectes (Insects)**
  un-SECTS

1) **abeille** (bee)
   ah-bay-YEH

2) **bourdon** (bumblebee)
   boor-DON

3) **guêpe** (wasp)
   gay-PEH

4) **scarabée** (beetle)
   ska-rah-BAY

5) **papillon** (butterfly)
   pah-pee-YON

6) **papillon de nuit** (moth)
   pah-pee-yon-deuh-NWEE

7) **libellule** (dragonfly)
   lee-BELULE

8) **coccinelle** (ladybug)
   cok-see-NELL

9) **luciole** (firefly)
   luh-see-OLE

10) **cafard** (cockroach)
    kah-FAR

11) **taon** (horsefly)
    TAN

12) **mouche** (fly)
    moo-CHEH

13) **moustique** (mosquito)
    moos-TEEK

14) **sauterelle** (grasshopper)
    so-t-REL

15) **grillon** (cricket)
    gree-YON

- **Arachnides (Arachnids)**
  ah-rak-KNEED

16) **scorpion** (scorpion)
    score-pee-YON

17) **araignée** (spider)
    ah-ray-NYAY

18) **veuve noire** (Southern black widow)
    veuh-ve-NWAR

Je déteste les araignées.
I hate spiders.

Je me suis fait piquer par une guêpe.
I got stung by a wasp.

Les coccinelles portent chance.
Ladybugs bring good luck.

LES MAMMIFÈRES I (MAMMALS I)

1) **chauve-souris** (bat)
chov-soo-REE

2) **ornithorynque** (platypus)
or-knee-toh-RHINK

3) **orque** (killer whale/orca)
ORK

4) **dauphin** (dolphin)
doh-FIN

5) **castor** (beaver)
kass-TOR

6) **marmotte** (groundhog)
mar-MOTT

7) **taupe** (mole)
toh-PEH

8) **écureuil** (squirrel)
hey-queue-reu-YEH

9) **belette** (weasel)
beh-LETT

10) **opossum** (possum/opossum)
oh-poss-HUM

11) **rat** (rat)
RAH

12) **lièvre** (hare)
lee-yeh-VREH

13) **blaireau** (badger)
blay-ROH

14) **mouflette** (skunk)
moof-LETTE

15) **léopard** (leopard)
lay-oh-PAR

Les vampires se transforment en chauve-souris.
Vampires turn into bats.

Il y a un écureuil rouge dans l'arbre.
There is a red squirrel in the tree.

Regarde, elle a un rat sur son épaule !
Look, she has a rat on her shoulder!

LES MAMMIFÈRES II (MAMMALS II)

1) **ours** (bear)
   oor-SS

2) **hyène** (hyena)
   hee-YEN

3) **chacal** (jackal)
   cha-KAL

4) **vache** (cow)
   vah-CHEH

5) **taureau** (bull)
   tow-ROW

6) **renard** (fox)
   reh-NAR

7) **buffle** (buffalo)
   buu-FFLEH

8) **élan** (elk/moose)
   hey-LAN

9) **mouton** (sheep)
   moo-TON

10) **chèvre** (goat)
    chey-VREH

11) **gazelle** (gazelle)
    gah-ZELL

12) **loup** (wolf)
    LOO

13) **singe** (monkey)
    ss-un-GEH

14) **bélier** (ram)
    bey-LIEY

15) **âne** (donkey)
    ah-NEH

Il ne faut jamais courir devant un ours.
Never run in front of a bear.

Le petit chaperon rouge s'est fait manger par le loup.
Little Red Riding Hood was eaten by a wolf.

Ma vache me donne du lait tous les jours.
My cow gives me milk every day.

POISSONS ET MOLLUSQUES (FISH AND MOLLUSKS)

- **Poissons (Fish)**
  pwa-ss-ON

1) **Requin-baleine** (whale shark)
   reh-k-un-bah-lay-NEH

2) **requin blanc** (white shark)
   reh-k-un-BLAN

3) **requin marteau** (hammerhead shark)
   reh-k-un-mar-TOW

4) **espadon** (swordfish/marlin)
   ess-pah-DON

5) **barracuda** (barracuda)
   bah-rah-coo-DAH

6) **poisson-globe** (pufferfish)
   pwa-ss-on-GLOBE

7) **poisson-chat** (catfish)
   pwa-ss-on-CHAH

8) **piranha** (piranha)
   pee-rah-NAH

9) **poisson volant** (flying fish)
   pwa-ss-on-voh-LAN

10) **murène** (moray eel)
    mu-ray-NAH

11) **raie manta** (manta ray)
    ray-man-TAH

12) **hippocampe** (seahorse)
    hee-poh-CAMP

- **Mollusques (Mollusks)**
  moh-LUSK

13) **calamar** (squid)
    kah-lah-MAR

14) **seiche** (cuttlefish)
    say-CHE

15) **poulpe** (octopus)
    pool-PEH

16) **huître** (oyster)
    hwee-TREH

17) **palourde** (clam)
    pah-loor-DEH

18) **nautile** (nautilus)
    no-tee-LEH

19) **escargot** (snail)
    es-car-GO

20) **limace** (slug)
    lee-mah-CEH

Attention aux requins blancs.
Beware of the white sharks.

Je déteste manger des huîtres.
I hate eating oysters.

Mon frère a pêché un énorme poisson-chat.
My brother caught a huge catfish.

LES VÊTEMENTS I (CLOTHING I)

1) **manteau de pluie** (raincoat)
   man-toh-deuh-PLWEE

2) **sweat à capuche** (hoodie)
   sweat-ah-cah-pu-CHEH

3) **veste** (jacket)
   VEST

4) **jeans** (jeans)
   JEANS

5) **caleçon** (boxer shorts)
   ka-leh-SON

6) **bottes** (boots)
   BOTT

7) **boucles d'oreilles** (earrings)
   boo-cleh-doh-ray-YEH

8) **pull** (sweater)
   PUUL

9) **collier** (necklace)
   col-YAY

10) **soutien-gorge** (bra)
    soo-tee-yen-gor-GEH

11) **leggings** (leggings)
    ley-GINS

12) **chaussettes** (socks)
    cho-ss-ETTE

13) **blouse/haut** (blouse/top)
    BLOOZ/OH

14) **bracelet** (bracelet)
    bra-ceh-LAY

15) **short** (shorts)
    SHORT

16) **culottes** (panties)
    queue-LOTT

17) **manteau** (coat)
    man-TOH

18) **robe** (dress)
    ROB

19) **sac à main** (purse)
    sak-ah-MUN

20) **sandales** (sandals)
    san-DAL

N'oublie pas ton manteau de pluie !
Do not forget your raincoat!

Il y a un trou dans ma chaussette.
There is a hole in my sock.

Si tu as froid, mets un pull.
If you are cold, wear a sweater.

LES VÊTEMENTS II (CLOTHING II)

1) **chapeau** (hat)
cha-POH

2) **smoking** (tuxedo/smoking)
smo-KING

3) **nœud papillon** (bow tie)
neuh-pah-pee-YON

4) **chaussures** (shoes)
cho-SSUR

5) **costume** (suit)
cos-TUM

6) **chemise** (shirt)
che-MIZ

7) **cravate** (tie)
krah-VAT

8) **mallette** (briefcase/case)
mah-LETT

9) **blouse à manches longues** (long-sleeved blouse)
blooz-ah-manch-LONG

10) **soutien-gorge de sport** (sports bra)
soo-tien-gorg-deuh-SPORT

11) **pantalon** (trousers/pants)
pan-ta-LONG

12) **ceinture** (belt)
sein-TUR

13) **bague** (ring)
BAG

14) **tee-shirt** (T-shirt)
tee-SHIRT

15) **jupe** (skirt)
JUUP

16) **écharpe** (scarf)
hé-SHARP

17) **montre** (watch)
MONTR

18) **pantalon cargo** (cargo pants)
pan-tah-lon-CARGO

19) **portefeuille** (wallet)
port-FEUIL

20) **parapluie** (umbrella)
pah-rah-PLWEE

L'argent est dans la mallette.
The money is in the briefcase.

Le soleil brille, tu dois mettre un chapeau.
The sun is shining, you must wear a hat.

J'ai perdu ma montre.
I have lost my watch.

LA MÉTÉO (THE WEATHER)

1) **ensoleillé** (sunny)
   an-so-lay-YAY

2) **chaud** (hot)
   CHO

3) **tempête de sable** (sandstorm)
   tempet-deuh-sah-BLEH

4) **nuageux** (cloudy)
   nu-ah-JEU

5) **chaud** (warm)
   CHO

6) **brumeux** (foggy/misty)
   brew-MEUH

7) **pluvieux** (rainy)
   plu-vee-YEUH

8) **frais** (cool)
   FRAY

9) **goutte de pluie** (raindrop)
   goot-deuh-PLWEE

10) **humide** (humid)
    hu-MID

11) **tempête** (storm)
    tem-PETTE

12) **éclairs** (lightning)
    hay-CLAIR

13) **venteux** (windy)
    ven-TEUH

14) **enneigé** (snowy)
    an-nay-GEY

15) **froid** (cold)
    FRWAH

16) **flocon de neige** (snowflake)
    flow-con-deuh-ney-GEH

Il fait très chaud à Dubaï.
It is very hot in Dubai.

J'ai froid.
I am cold.

Nous ne pouvons pas aller dans le désert à cause d'une tempête de sable.
We cannot go into the desert because of a sandstorm.

LES SAISONS – LE PRINTEMPS (THE SEASONS – SPRING)

1) **jardin** (garden)
jar-DIN

2) **fleurir** (blossom)
fleuh-REER

3) **pique-nique** (picnic)
pik-NIK

4) **parc** (park)
PARK

5) **balade à vélo** (bike ride)
bal-ah-de-ah-vay-LOH

6) **limonade** (lemonade)
lee-mon-ah-DEH

7) **vide-greniers** (garage sale)
veed-greh-NYAY

8) **road trip** (road trip)
road-TRIP

9) **peindre des cailloux** (to paint rocks)
paindr-day-cah-YOU

10) **planter des fleurs** (to plant some flowers)
plan-tay-day-FLEUR

11) **faire voler un cerf-volant** (to fly a kite)
fair-volay-un-ser-VOLAN

12) **aller à un barbecue** (to attend a barbecue)
allay-ah-un-bar-beh-CUE

Samedi, nous allons faire un pique-nique dans le parc.
Saturday, we are going to have a picnic in the park.

Je rêve de faire un road trip en Amérique.
I dream of going on a road trip through America.

Nous aimons faire des balades à vélo dans les Alpes.
We love bike rides in the Alps.

LES SAISONS – L'ÉTÉ (THE SEASONS – SUMMER)

1) **aller camper** (to go camping)
   allay-cam-PAY

2) **parc aquatique** (water park)
   park-aqua-TEEK

3) **activités extérieures** (outdoor activities
   actee-vee-tay-extay-ree-EUR

4) **piscine** (swimming pool)
   pee-see-NEH

5) **nager** (to swim)
   nah-JAY

6) **se faire bronzer** (to get tanned)
   she-fair-bronz-AY

7) **crème solaire** (sunscreen)
   crem-soh-LAIR

8) **insectifuge** (insect repellent)
   un-sec-tee-FUGE

9) **lac** (lake)
   LAK

10) **maître-nageur** (lifesaver/lifeguard)
    may-treh-nah-GEUR

11) **château de sable** (sandcastle)
    chah-tow-deuh-sah-BLEH

12) **partir en randonnée** (to go on a hike)
    par-teer-en-ran-doh-NAY

Le lac d'Annecy est magnifique.
The Annecy Lake is beautiful.

J'adore me faire bronzer sur la plage.
I love to tan on the beach.

N'oublie pas ta crème solaire !
Do not forget your sunscreen!

QUIZ #2

Use arrows to match the corresponding translations:

a. horsefly

b. mole

c. king cobra

d. coat

e. socks

f. Komodo dragon

g. tie

h. slug

i. ring

j. snail

k. sunny

l. beetle

m. bat

n. warm

o. necklace

p. butterfly

1. ensoleillé

2. chaussettes

3. bague

4. scarabée

5. taupe

6. chauve-souris

7. chaud

8. cobra royal

9. manteau

10. taon

11. collier

12. escargot

13. dragon de Komodo

14. papillon

15. cravate

16. limace

Fill in the blank spaces with the options below (use each word only once):

Phil est professeur de maternelle. La semaine dernière, il a amené la classe visiter une ferme. La météo avait annoncé de la pluie, mais il a fait très _____. C'était une journée très _____. Phil avait mis un _____, des _____ de marche et un gros _____. Malheureusement, il s'est senti inconfortable toute la journée. Pendant la visite de la ferme, les enfants ont vu des cochons, des chevaux et des _____. Il y avait aussi une ruche avec des centaines d'_____. Par contre, il y avait aussi des _____ et l'une d'elle a piqué Phil !

jeans	abeilles
chaussures	ensoleillée
guêpes	vaches
chaud	manteau

LES SAISONS – L'AUTOMNE (THE SEASONS – FALL/AUTUMN)

1) **les feuilles changeantes** (changing leaves)
   ley-feuiy-chan-JANTE

2) **ramasser des feuilles** (to collect leaves)
   rah-mah-say-day-FEUIY

3) **citrouille** (pumpkin)
   see-troo-YEH

4) **sculpter une citrouille** (to carve a pumpkin)
   scul-ptay-une-see-troo-YEH

5) **ramasser des pommes** (apple picking)
   rah-mah-say-day-POM

6) **costume d'Halloween** (Halloween costume)
   costum-d-Hallo-WEEN

7) **bonbons d'Halloween** (Halloween candy)
   bon-bon-dah-llo-weenWEEN

8) **bougies épicées** (spiced candles)
   boo-jee-hay-pee-SAY

9) **dîner de Thanksgiving** (Thanksgiving dinner)
   dee-nay-deuh-Thanks-gi-VING

10) **couverture en laine** (wool blanket)
    coo-ver-tur-en-lay-NEH

11) **rôtir des Chamallows** (to roast marshmallows)
    roh-teer-day-cha-mah-LOW

12) **décorer le jardin** (to decorate the yard)
    day-co-ray-leuh-jar-DIN

J'ai sculpté une citrouille pour Halloween.
I carved a pumpkin for Halloween.

J'ai acheté des bougies épicées pour Noël.
I bought spiced candles for Christmas.

En décembre, je commence à décorer le jardin.
In December, I start to decorate the yard.

LES SAISONS – L'HIVER (THE SEASONS – WINTER)

1) **chocolat chaud** (hot cocoa/hot chocolate)
   cho-co-lah-CHO

2) **luge** (sled)
   lu-GEH

3) **mouffles** (mittens)
   moo-FLEH

4) **veste matelassée** (puffy jacket)
   vest-mah-the-lah-SAY

5) **soupe** (soup)
   SOUP

6) **biscuits en pain d'épices** (gingerbread cookies)
   bees-cwee-oh-jun-JAMBREH

7) **fenêtre gelée** (frosty window)
   feh-netr-geh-LAY

8) **pomme de pin** (pinecone)
   pom-deuh-PIN

9) **patin à glace** (ice skating)
   pah-t-un-ah-GLASS

10) **ski** (ski)
    SKI

11) **patinoire** (ice rink)
    pah-tee-NWAR

12) **boule de neige** (snowball)
    bool-deuh-ney-GEH

J'aime boire un chocolat chaud près du feu.
I love to drink hot chocolate near the fire.

Je fais du ski depuis l'âge de 4 ans.
I started skiing at the age of 4.

La soupe est prête.
The soup is ready.

LE TEMPS (TIME)

1) **fuseau horaire** (time zone)
fu-zo-oh-RAIR

2) **seconde** (second)
seh-GONDE

3) **minute** (minute)
mee-NUUT

4) **heure** (hour)
HEUR

5) **jour** (day)
JOOR

6) **semaine** (week)
seh-MAIN

7) **quinzaine** (fortnight)
kain-ZAIN

8) **mois** (month)
MWA

9) **année** (year)
ANAY

10) **aurore** (dawn)
oh-ROR

11) **matin** (morning)
mah-t-UN

12) **midi** (noon/midday)
mee-DEE

13) **après-midi** (afternoon)
apray-mee-DEE

14) **crépuscule** (dusk)
cray-pus-cu-LEH

15) **nuit** (night)
NWEE

16) **minuit** (midnight)
mee-NWEE

17) **date** (date)
day-TEH

18) **calendrier** (calendar)
kah-lan-dree-YAY

Ma fille se réveille souvent la nuit.
My daughter wakes up often at night.

Quelle est ta date de naissance ?
When is your birthday?

Nous t'attendons pour manger à midi.
We are waiting for you at 12 p.m. for lunch.

① ② ③ ④

⑤ TODAY APRIL 10

MAY 2020 ⑧

2020 ⑥

SUN	MON	TUE	WED	THU	FRI	SAT

⑦

SUN	MON	TUE	WED	THU	FRI	SAT
2	3	4	5	6	7	8
9	10	11	12	13	14	15

2020 ⑨

JAN	FEB	MARCH	APRIL
MAY	JUNE	JULY	AUG
SEPT	OCT	NOV	DEC

⑰ MAY 1

⑱ APRIL 2020

SUN	MON	TUE	WED	THU	FRI	SAT

⑩ ⑪ ⑫ ⑬ ⑭ ⑮ ⑯

LA MAISON (THE HOUSE)

1) **grenier** (attic)
   greh-nee-YAY

2) **toit** (roof)
   TWA

3) **plafond** (ceiling)
   plah-FON

4) **cheminée** (chimney)
   cheh-mee-NAY

5) **mur** (wall)
   MUUR

6) **balcon** (balcony)
   bahl-CON

7) **porche** (porch)
   por-CHEH

8) **fenêtre** (window)
   feh-nay-TREH

9) **volets** (shutters)
   vo-LAY

10) **porte** (door)
    PORT

11) **escaliers** (stairs)
    ess-kah-lee-YAY

12) **barrière** (banister)
    bar-ee-AIR

13) **sol** (floor)
    SOL

14) **sous-sol** (basement)
    soo-SOL

15) **jardin** (backyard)
    jar-DUN

16) **garage** (garage)
    gah-rah-GEH

17) **allée** (driveway)
    ALLAY

18) **clôture** (fence/picket fence)
    cloh-TUR

19) **boîte aux lettres** (mailbox)
    bwat-oh-lay-TREH

20) **couloir** (hallway/corridor)
    cool-WAR

Il y a des toiles d'araignées au plafond.
There are cobwebs on the ceiling.

Votre jardin est très beau.
Your backyard is very beautiful.

Je suis tombé dans les escaliers.
I fell down the stairs.

DANS LA CUISINE (KITCHEN ITEMS)

1) **cuisinière** (stove)
cwee-zee-nee-YAIR

2) **four à micro-ondes** (microwave oven)
foor-ah-mee-croh-ONDE

3) **four grille-pain** (toaster oven)
foor-gree-yeh-PIN

4) **mixeur électrique** (electric mixer)
mix-eur-hey-layk-TREEK

5) **mixeur** (blender)
mix-EUR

6) **grille-pain** (toaster)
gree-yeh-PIN

7) **machine à café** (coffee maker)
machine-ah-cah-FAY

8) **réfrigérateur** (fridge)
ray-fray-gee-rah-TEUR

9) **garde-manger** (pantry)
guard-man-JAY

10) **placard** (cupboard)
plah-CAR

11) **moule à gâteaux** (cake pan)
mool-ah-gah-TOW

12) **poêle à frire** (frying pan)
pwal-ah-FREER

13) **casserole** (pot)
cass-ROLL

14) **emporte-pièces** (cookie cutters)
am-port-pee-ACE

15) **bol mélangeur** (mixing bowl)
bol-may-lange-EUR

16) **passoire** (colander)
pass-WAR

17) **tamis** (strainer)
tah-MEE

18) **rouleau à pâtisseri**e (rolling pin)
roo-loh-ah-pah-teess-REE

19) **gant isolant** (oven mitt)
gan-ee-zo-LAN

20) **tablier** (apron)
tah-blee-YAY

J'ai uilisé un mixeur pour faire un smoothie.
I used a blender to make a smoothie.

Va chercher un yaourt au réfrigérateur.
Go get a yogurt in the fridge.

J'ai étalé la pâte avec un rouleau à pâtisserie.
I rolled the pastry with a rolling pin.

DANS LA CHAMBRE (BEDROOM ITEMS)

1) **lit** (bed)
LEE

2) **matelas** (mattress)
mah-teh-LAH

3) **literie** (bedding/bed linen)
leet-REE

4) **oreiller** (pillow)
oh-ray-YAY

5) **draps** (sheets)
DRAH

6) **couverture** (blanket)
coo-ver-TUR

7) **housse** (spread)
HOUSE

8) **taie d'oreiller** (pillowcase)
tay-doh-ray-YAY

9) **table de nuit** (nightstand)
tah-bleh-deuh-NWEE

10) **horloge de table** (table clock)
or-lo-geh-deuh-tah-BLEH

11) **lampe de chevet** (table light)
lamp-deuh-che-VAY

12) **armoire** (closet)
arm-WAR

13) **chaise à bascule** (rocking chair)
chaiz-ah-bass-CULEH

14) **lampe** (lamp)
LAMP

15) **miroir** (mirror)
mee-RWAR

16) **commode** (dresser)
coh-MODE

17) **rideau** (curtain)
ree-DOH

18) **berceau** (cradle/crib)
bear-SOW

19) **mobile** (crib mobile)
moh-BILL

20) **ceintre** (hanger)
sain-TREH

Je vais changer les draps du lit.
I am going to change the bedsheets.

Le bébé est dans son berceau.
The baby is in his crib.

Ce matelas est trop dur pour moi.
This mattress is too hard for me.

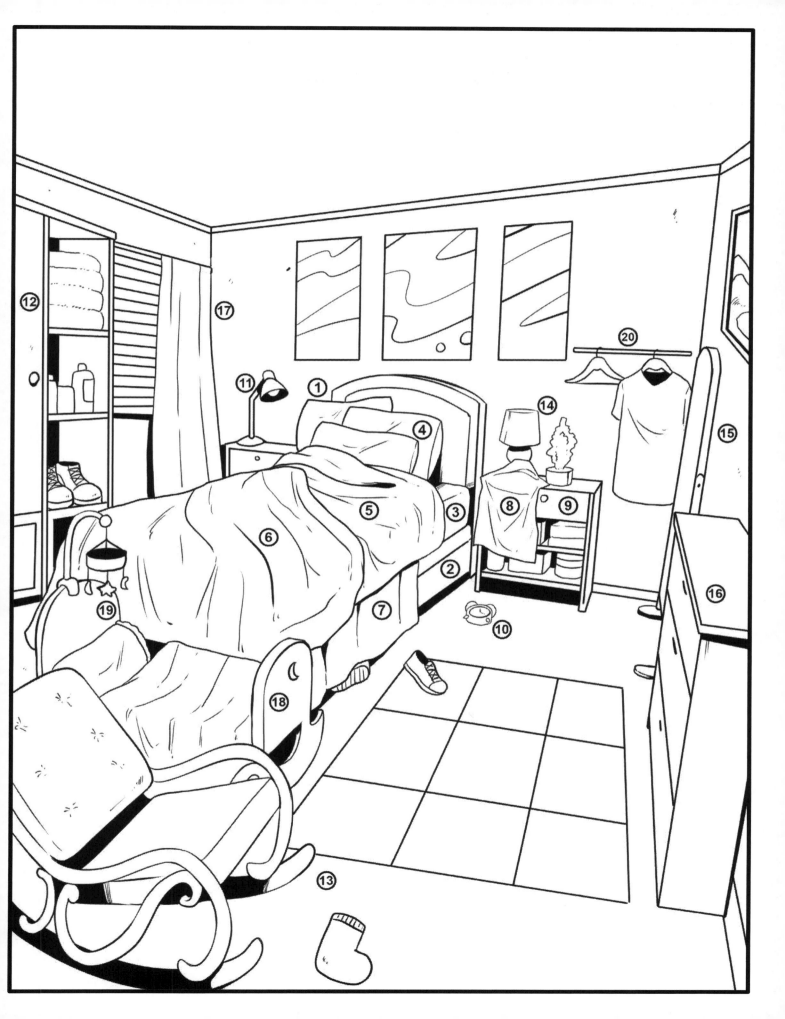

DANS LA SALLE DE BAINS (BATHROOM ITEMS)

1) **rideau de douche** (shower curtain)
   ree-doh-deuh-DOUCHE

2) **serviette** (towel)
   ser-vee-yetteYETTE

3) **porte-serviettes** (towel rack)
   port-ser-vee-YETTE

4) **petite serviette** (hand towel)
   petite-ser-vee-YETTE

5) **baignoire** (bathtub)
   bay-NWAR

6) **douche** (shower)
   DOUCHE

7) **toilettes** (toilet/WC)
   twa-LETTE

8) **lavabo** (sink/washbasin)
   lah-vah-BOH

9) **robinet** (faucet/tap)
   roh-bee-NAY

10) **tapis de bain** (bathmat)
    tah-pee-deuh-b-UN

11) **armoire à pharmacie** (medicine cabinet)
    arm-war-ah-far-mah-SEE

12) **dentifrice** (toothpaste)
    den-tee-free-SSE

13) **brosse à dents** (toothbrush)
    bross-ah-DEN

14) **shampooing** (shampoo)
    shamp-oo-UN

15) **peigne** (comb)
    pay-GNEH

16) **savon** (soap)
    sah-VON

17) **mousse à raser** (shaving foam)
    mouss-ah-rah-ZAY

18) **rasoir** (razor/shaver)
    rah-ZWAR

19) **papier toilettes** (toilet paper)
    pah-pee-yay-twa-LETTE

20) **ventouse** (plunger)
    ven-TOOZ

21) **brosse à toilettes** (toilet brush)
    bross-deuh-twa-LETTE

22) **corbeille** (wastebasket)
    kor-bay-YEH

Il n'y a plus de papier toilettes !
There is no more toilet paper!

Mets la serviette sur le porte-serviettes.
Place the towel on the towel rack.

N'oublie pas de fermer le robinet.
Do not forget to turn off the tap.

DANS LE SALON (LIVING ROOM ITEMS)

1) **meuble** (furniture)
meh-BLEH

2) **chaise** (chair)
CHAYZ

3) **divan** (sofa)
dee-VAN

4) **canapé** (couch)
lah-nah-PAY

5) **coussin** (cushion)
coo-ss-UN

6) **table basse** (coffee table)
tah-bleh-BASS

7) **cendrier** (ashtray)
san-dree-YAY

8) **vase** (vase)
vah-ZE

9) **décorations** (ornaments)
day-cor-ha-sse-YON

10) **bibliothèque** (bookshelf/bookcase)
bee-blee-oh-TEK

11) **porte-magazines** (magazine holder)
port-mah-gah-ZEENE

12) **chaîne hifi** (stereo)
chain-hee-FEE

13) **haut-parleurs** (speakers)
oh-par-LEUR

14) **cheminée** (fireplace)
cheh-mee-NAY

15) **chandelier** (chandelier)
chan-deuh-lee-YAY

16) **lampe** (lamp)
LAMP

17) **ampoule** (light bulb)
am-POOL

18) **horloge** (wall clock)
or-LOJE

19) **tableau** (painting)
tah-BLOH

20) **télévision** (TV/television)
tay-lay-veez-YON

21) **télécommande** (remote control)
tay-lay-coh-MANDE

22) **console de jeux vidéo** (video game console)
consol-deuh-jeu-vee-day-OH

Je passe trop de temps devant la télévision.
I spend too much time in front of the TV.

J'ai acheté une console de jeux à mon mari pour Noël.
I bought my husband a video game console for Christmas.

J'ai bientôt fini mon premier tableau.
I have nearly finished my first painting.

DANS LA SALLE À MANGER (DINING ROOM ITEMS)

1) **table à manger** (dining table)
tah-bleh-ah-man-GEY

2) **nappe** (tablecloth)
NAP

3) **centre de table** (centerpiece)
san-treh-deuh-tah-BLEH

4) **napperon** (placemat)
nah-per-ON

5) **assiette** (plate)
ass-YETTE

6) **serviette** (napkin)
ser-vee-YETTE

7) **couteau** (knife)
coo-TOW

8) **fourchette** (fork)
four-CHETTE

9) **cuillère** (spoon)
cwee-YER

10) **pichet** (pitcher/jar)
pee-CHAY

11) **verre** (glass)
VER

12) **tasse** (mug/cup)
TAHSS

13) **salière** (saltshaker)
sah-lee-YER

14) **poivrière** (pepper shaker)
pwa-vree-YER

15) **plateau** (tray)
plah-TOW

16) **boisson** (drink/beverage)
bwa-SON

17) **nourriture** (food)
noo-ree-TURE

18) **en-cas** (snack)
en-KAH

Je vais t'amener le petit-déjeuner sur un plateau.
I will bring you breakfast on a tray.

Quel centre de table as-tu choisi pour ton mariage ?
Which centerpiece have you chosen for your wedding?

Tu veux une boisson ?
Do you want a drink?

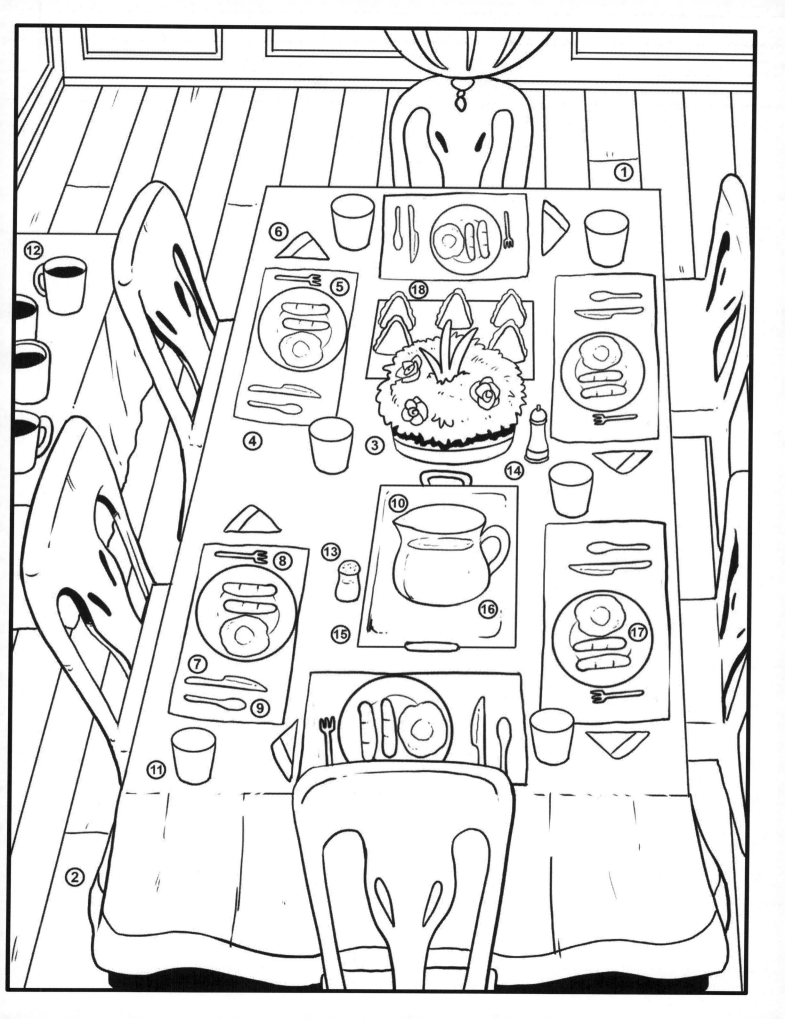

QUIZ #3

Use arrows to match the corresponding translations:

a. morning

b. pumpkin

c. door

d. Halloween costume

e. pillow

f. afternoon

g. sled

h. apron

i. ice rink

j. towel rack

k. wall

l. closet

m. window

n. fireplace

o. snowball

p. toaster

1. fenêtre

2. armoire

3. luge

4. mur

5. tablier

6. boule de neige

7. oreiller

8. costume d'Halloween

9. porte

10. grille-pain

11. après-midi

12. porte-serviettes

13. patinoire

14. citrouille

15. cheminée

16. matin

Fill in the blank spaces with the options below (use each word only once):

L'automne, c'est ma saison préférée. Chaque année, j'attends octobre avec impatience pour _____ et aussi mon _____. Ma famille et moi aimons _____ et les placer dans toute la maison. J'en met toujours une devant la _____, elles ressemblent à de petites _____ effrayantes ! Le 31 octobre, c'est Halloween. Nous allons chercher des bonbons chez les voisins. Après ça, vers _____, nous allumons des _____, et nous nous relaxons dans le _____ en buvant un bon _____. En général, mon frère joue à la _____. En novembre, c'est le moment de faire du _____ et d'aller à la _____ de notre ville. J'adore ça !

balcon

chocolat chaud

minuit

lampe

bougies épicées

console de jeux vidéo

creuser les citrouilles

canapé

décorer le jardin

ski

patinoire

cheminée

LE JARDIN (THE GARDEN/THE BACKYARD)

1) **jardinier** (gardener)
jar-dee-NYAY

2) **remise** (shed)
reh-MEEZ

3) **buisson** (bush)
bwee-SON

4) **pelouse** (lawn)
peh-LOOSE

5) **herbe** (grass)
HERB

6) **fleur** (flower)
FLEUR

7) **tuyau d'arrosage** (garden hose)
twee-yo-dah-roh-zah-GE

8) **arrosoir** (watering can)
ah-row-ZWAR

9) **pot de fleurs** (flowerpot)
poh-deuh-FLEUR

10) **gants de jardinage** (gardening gloves)
gan-deuh-jar-dee-nah-JE

11) **pelle** (shovel)
PEL

12) **râteau** (rake)
rah-TOW

13) **fourche** (gardening fork)
foor-CHEH

14) **sécateur** (pruners/pruning shears)
say-kah-TEUR

15) **truelle** (garden trowel)
true-ELLE

16) **robinet** (tap)
roh-bee-NAY

17) **brouette** (wheelbarrow)
broo-ETTE

18) **tondeuse** (lawn mower)
ton-deuh-ZEH

19) **lanterne** (lantern)
lan-TERN

20) **vigne** (vine)
vee-GNE

Une vigne pousse dans mon jardin.
A vine grows in my garden.

J'ai mis tous mes outils dans la remise.
I have put all my tools in the shed.

La brouette est pleine de feuilles mortes.
The wheelbarrow is full of dead leaves.

LA BUANDERIE (THE CLEANING ROOM)

1) **machine à laver** (washing machine)
machine-ah-LAVAY

2) **sèche-linge** (dryer)
sey-cheh-lin-JE

3) **fer à repasser** (iron)
fer-ah-reh-pah-SSAY

4) **table de repassage** (ironing board)
tah-bleh-deuh-reh-pah-SSAJE

5) **lessive** (laundry soap)
sah-von-ah-lin-JE

6) **détergent** (laundry detergent)
less-ee-VEH

7) **adoucissant** (fabric softener)
ah-dou-see-SSAN

8) **corbeille à linge** (laundry basket)
kor-beye-ah-lin-JE

9) **linge sale** (dirty clothes)
lin-je-sah-LEH

10) **linge propre** (clean laundry)
lin-je-proh-PREH

11) **balai** (broom)
bah-LAY

12) **pelle à poussière** (dust pan)
pel-ah-poo-SSYERE

13) **gants en caoutchouc** (rubber gloves)
gan-en-kah-oo-TCHOO

14) **éponge** (sponge)
hey-PONJE

15) **bac en plastique** (plastic tub)
bcac-en-plass-TEEK

16) **serpillière** (mop)
ser-pee-YERE

17) **seau** (bucket)
SO

18) **chiffon nettoyant** (cleaning cloths)
chee-fon-nay-twa-YAN

19) **brosse à récurer** (scrub brush)
bross-deuh-lah-vah-JE

20) **javel** (bleach)
jah-VEL

21) **désinfectant** (disinfectant)
dey-sin-fec-TAN

22) **poubelle** (garbage can)
poo-BEL

Je déteste faire la lessive.
I hate doing the laundry.

Tu dois passer la serpillière.
You must mop the floor.

Tu peux utiliser de l'adoucissant dans la machine à laver.
You can use fabric softener in the washing machine.

L'ÉCOLE / L'UNIVERSITÉ (THE SCHOOL/THE UNIVERSITY)

1) **professeur** (teacher)
pro-fess-EUR

2) **étudiant** (student)
hey-tu-dee-YAN

3) **salle de classe** (classroom)
sal-deuh-KLASS

4) **casier** (locker)
kah-zee-YAY

5) **tableau d'affichage** (bulletin board)
tah-blow-dah-fee-CHAJE

6) **feuille de papier** (sheet of paper)
feuye-deuh-pah-pee-YAY

7) **livre** (book)
lee-VREH

8) **carnet de notes** (notebook)
kar-nay-deuh-NOTE

9) **colle** (glue)
COL

10) **ciseaux** (scissors)
see-ZOH

11) **crayon à papier** (pencil)
cray-yon-deuh-pah-pee-YAY

12) **gomme** (eraser)
GOM

13) **taille-crayon** (pencil sharpener)
tah-yeh-cray-YON

14) **stylo** (pen)
stee-LOH

15) **marqueur** (marker)
mar-KEUR

16) **surligneur** (highlighter)
sur-lee-GNEUR

17) **enveloppe** (envelope)
en-ve-LOP

18) **presse-papier** (clipboard)
press-pah-pee-YAY

19) **tableau noir** (blackboard)
tah-blow-NWAR

20) **calculatrice** (calculator)
kal-ku-lah-tree-SS

21) **règle** (ruler)
ray-GLEH

22) **agrafeuse** (stapler)
ah-grah-feu-ZEH

23) **trousse** (pouch/pencil case)
TROOSS

24) **bureau d'écolier** (school desk)
bureau-day-col-YAY

25) **table** (table)
tah-BLEH

26) **ordinateur portable** (laptop)
or-dee-nah-teur-por-tah-BLEH

Ce calcul est trop compliqué sans calculatrice.
This calculation is too complicated without a calculator.

Utilise ta gomme pour corriger ton erreur.
Use your eraser to correct your mistake.

Je ne trouve pas mon taille-crayon.
I cannot find my pencil sharpener.

LE BUREAU (THE OFFICE)

1) **patron** (boss)
   pah-TRON

2) **supérieur** (superior)
   su-pay-ree-YEUR

3) **employé** (employee)
   em-plwa-YAY

4) **directeur** (CEO/president)
   dee-rec-TEUR

5) **partenaire commercial** (business partner)
   par-the-nair-koh-mer-see-YAL

6) **collègue** (colleague)
   koh-LEG

7) **collaborateur** (co-worker)
   koh-lah-bo-rah-TEUR

8) **secrétaire** (secretary)
   sec-ray-TAIR

9) **compartiment** (cubicle)
   con-par-tee-MAN

10) **chaise de bureau** (swivel chair)
    chaiz-deuh-bu-ROH

11) **bureau** (desk)
    bu-ROH

12) **ordinateur** (computer)
    or-dee-nah-TEUR

13) **imprimante** (printer)
    un-pree-MANTE

14) **fournitures de bureau** (office supplies)
    foor-nee-tur-deuh-bu-ROH

15) **tampon en caoutchouc** (rubber stamp)
    tampon-an-kah-oo-TCHOO

16) **distributeur de bande adhésive** (tape dispenser)
    dis-tree-bu-teur-deuh-band-ah-day-ZEEV

17) **classeur** (folder)
    klah-SSEUR

18) **meuble classeur** (filing cabinet)
    meuh-bleh-klah-SSEUR

19) **fax** (fax)
    FAX

20) **téléphone** (telephone)
    tay-lay-PHONE

J'aime beaucoup ma nouvelle collègue.
I really like my new colleague.

Donnez votre numéro à ma secrétaire.
Give your number to my secretary.

Plus personne n'utilise de fax !
No one uses a fax anymore!

LES MÉTIERS (PROFESSIONS/OCCUPATIONS)

1) **ingénieur** (engineer)
   un-jey-knee-YEUR

2) **astronaute** (astronaut)
   ass-troh-NOT

3) **pilote** (pilot)
   pee-LOT

4) **juge** (judge)
   ju-GEH

5) **pompier** (firefighter)
   pom-pee-YAY

6) **policier** (police officer)
   poh-lee-see-YAY

7) **cuisinier** (chef)
   qwee-zee-knee-YAY

8) **chef d'orchestre** (conductor)
   chef-dor-kess-TRE

9) **professeur** (professor)
   pro-fess-EUR

10) **danseur** (dancer)
    dan-ss-EUR

11) **homme d'affaires** (businessman)
    hom-dah-FAIR

12) **entraîneur animalier**(animal trainer)
    en-tray-neur-dah-knee-MAL

Quand j'étais petit, je voulais devenir pilote.
When I was a kid, I wanted to be a pilot.

Il deviendra un bon homme d'affaires.
He will become a good businessman.

Appelle les pompiers !
Call the firefighters!

LES MOYENS DE TRANSPORT (MEANS OF TRANSPORT)

1) **vélo** (bike/bicycle)
vay-LOH

2) **moto** (motorcycle/motorbike)
moh-TOH

3) **motoneige** (snowmobile)
moh-toh-ney-JE

4) **voiture** (car/automobile)
vwah-TUR

5) **bus** (bus)
BUS

6) **camion** (truck)
kah-me-YON

7) **métro** (subway)
may-TROH

8) **train** (train)
tr-unUN

9) **jet ski** (jet ski)
jet-SKEE

10) **bateau** (boat)
bah-TOW

11) **bateau de croisière** (cruise ship)
bah-tow-deuh-crwah-zee-YAIR

12) **sous-marin** (submarine)
soo-mar-UN

13) **dirigeable** (blimp/Zeppelin)
dee-ree-jah-BLE

14) **mongolfière** (hot-air balloon)
mon-gol-fee-YAIR

15) **avion** (plane/airplane)
ah-vee-YON

16) **hélicoptère** (helicopter/chopper)
hey-lee-cop-TER

17) **station spatiale** (space shuttle)
sta-see-yon-spa-see-YAL

Tu vas prendre le bus ou ta voiture ?
Are you going to take the bus or your car?

J'ai peur en avion.
I am scared of flying.

Nous avons réservé des vacances sur un bateau de croisière.
We have booked a holiday on a cruise ship.

LES PAYSAGES (LANDSCAPES)

1) **montagnes** (mountain)
mon-tah-GNE

2) **forêt tropicale** (tropical rainforest)
foh-ray-tro-pee-KAL

3) **désert** (desert)
day-ZER

4) **volcan** (volcano)
vol-CAN

5) **falaise** (cliff)
fah-LAYZ

6) **plage** (beach)
plah-JE

7) **forêt** (forest)
foh-RAY

8) **grotte** (cave)
GROTT

9) **geyser** (geyser)
jay-ZAIR

10) **cascade** (waterfall/falls)
chut-DOH

11) **rivière** (river)
ree-vee-YAIR

12) **ruines anciennes** (ancient ruins)
ru-eene-an-see-YENNE

Je me suis perdu dans la forêt.
I got lost in the forest.

Les meilleures vacances sont à la montagne.
The best holidays are spent in the mountains.

Il faut traverser la rivière.
We must cross the river.

LES SPORTS I (SPORTS I)

1) **tir à l'arc** (archery)
   teer-ah-LARC

2) **boxe** (boxing)
   BOX

3) **cyclisme** (cycling)
   see-kleess-MEH

4) **escrime** (fencing)
   ess-kree-MEH

5) **football** (football/soccer)
   foot-BALL

6) **rugby** (rugby)
   rug-BEE

7) **tennis de table** (table tennis/ping-pong)
   tay-nees-deuh-tah-bleh/ping-PONG

8) **volley** (volleyball)
   voh-LAY

9) **musculation** (weightlift)
   mus-cu-lah-see-YON

10) **patinage** (skating)
    pah-tee-nah-JE

11) **sports paralympiques** (paralympic sports)
    spor-pah-rah-limp-PEEK

12) **baseball** (baseball)
    base-BALL

13) **basket** (basketball)
    bas-KET

J'admire beaucoup les joueurs de rugby.
I really admire rugby players.

Je vais à la salle de sport pour faire de la musculation.
I go to the gym to do weightlifting.

Les Français adorent le cyclisme.
French people love cycling.

LES SPORTS II (SPORTS II)

1) **badminton** (badminton)
bad-min-TON

2) **gymnastique** (gymnastics)
gym-nas-TEEK

3) **aviron** (rowing)
ah-vee-RON

4) **escalade** (sport climbing)
ess-kah-lah-DEH

5) **surf** (surfing)
SURF

6) **tennis** (tennis)
tay-NEES

7) **trampoline** (trampoline)
tram-poh-LEENE

8) **lutte** (wrestling)
LUTE

9) **ski** (skiing)
SKEE

10) **bobsleigh** (skeleton)
bob-SLAY

11) **patinage artistique** (figure skating)
pah-tee-nah-je-ar-tees-TEEK

12) **natation** (swimming)
nah-ta-see-YON

13) **waterpolo** (water polo)
water-poh-LO

14) **hockey** (hockey)
ho-KEY

L'aviron est très populaire en Angleterre.
Rowing is very popular in England.

Serena Williams est la meilleure joueuse de tennis.
Serena Williams is the best tennis player.

Je ne connais pas les règles du waterpolo.
I do not know the rules of water polo.

NOËL (CHRISTMAS DAY)

1) **gui** (mistletoe)
GEE

2) **guirlande** (garland)
geer-LAND

3) **sapin de noël** (Christmas tree)
sah-pin-deuh-noh-EL

4) **décorations de noël** (Christmas decorations)
day-co-rah-see-yon-deuh-noh-EL

5) **cadeaux de noël** (Christmas gifts/presents)
lah-doh-deuh-noh-EL

6) **repas de noël** (Christmas dinner)
reh-pa-deuh-noh-EL

7) **sucre d'orge** (candy cane)
sucre-dor-JE

8) **bonhomme en pain d'épice** (gingerbread man)
bon-hom-an-pin-day-PEACE

9) **elfe de noël** (Christmas elf)
elf-deuh-noh-EL

10) **bonnet de noël** (Christmas hat)
cha-pow-deuh-noh-EL

11) **Père Noël** (Santa Claus)
pair-noh-EL

12) **traîneau du Père Noël** (Santa's sleigh)
tray-no-duh-pair-noh-EL

13) **étoile de noël** (Christmas star)
hey-twal-deuh-noh-EL

14) **bonhomme de neige** (snowman)
bon-hom-deuh-nay-JE

15) **bougies** (candles)
boo-JEE

Nous mangerons du saumon pour le repas de Noël.
We will eat salmon for Christmas dinner.

Le Père Noël passe par la cheminée.
Santa Claus enters through the chimney.

J'ai acheté un sapin de Noël artificiel.
I bought an artificial Christmas tree.

QUIZ #4

Use arrows to match the corresponding translations:

a. engineer

b. printer

c. wheelbarrow

d. mop

e. colleague

f. gardener

g. bike

h. cave

i. plane

j. calculator

k. firefighter

l. boat

m. dirty laundry

n. washing machine

o. rake

p. classroom

1. pompier

2. calculatrice

3. salle de classe

4. linge sale

5. machine à laver

6. râteau

7. imprimante

8. avion

9. brouette

10. jardinier

11. collègue

12. vélo

13. serpillère

14. grotte

15. ingénieur

16. bateau

Fill in the blank spaces with the options below (use each word only once):

Gérald est _____ en ingénierie civile à l'université de Nantes. Il est en troisième année. Plus tard, il veut devenir _____ ou _____. Son but, c'est de devenir riche et de voyager le monde. Il rêve de jouer au _____ sur une _____ des Caraïbes, d'acheter son propre _____ ou bien de faire du _____ sur la mer. Son _____ favori, c'est Mr Rendal. Il est très intelligent et charismatique. Gérald espère lui ressembler plus tard. Mais pour le moment, il doit se rendre à la laverie pour utiliser la _____ et laver son _____. Avant cela, il doit aller au supermarché pour acheter de la _____ et de l'_____ car il n'en a plus.

professeur	linge sale
lessive	ingénieur
volley	jet ski
plage	machine à laver
assouplissant	étudiant
homme d'affaire	bateau

INSTRUMENTS DE MUSIQUE (MUSICAL INSTRUMENTS)

1) **guitare acoustique** (acoustic guitar)
gee-tar-ah-coos-TEEK

2) **guitare électrique** (electric guitar)
gee-tar-elec-TREEK

3) **guitare basse** (bass guitar)
gee-tar-BASS

4) **batterie** (drums)
bah-the-REE

5) **piano** (piano)
pee-ya-NO

6) **trompette** (trumpet)
trom-PET

7) **harmonica** (harmonica)
har-mo-nee-KAH

8) **flûte** (flute)
FLUT

9) **clarinette** (clarinet)
kla-ree-NET

10) **harpe** (harp)
HARP

11) **cornemuse** (bagpipes)
kor-ne-MUSE

12) **violoncelle** (cello)
vee-yo-lon-SEL

13) **violon** (violin)
vee-yo-LON

14) **saxophone** (saxophone)
sax-oh-PHONE

J'ai commencé à prendre des cours de piano.
I have started taking piano lessons.

La harpe est mon instrument préféré.
The harp is my favorite instrument.

Jimmy Hendrix était un génie de la guitare.
Jimmy Hendrix was a guitar genius.

LES FRUITS (FRUITS)

1) **fraise** (strawberry)
   fray-ZE

2) **papaye** (papaya)
   pah-pah-YEH

3) **prune** (plum)
   PRUNE

4) **melon** (melon)
   meh-LON

5) **pastèque** (watermelon)
   pass-TEK

6) **banane** (banana)
   bah-nah-NE

7) **mangue** (mango)
   man-GUE

8) **pêche** (peach)
   pay-CHE

9) **framboise** (raspberry)
   fram-bwa-ZEH

10) **orange** (orange)
    oh-RANJE

11) **citron** (lemon)
    see-TRON

12) **ananas** (pineapple)
    ah-nah-NASS

13) **citron vert** (lime)
    see-tron-VER

14) **raisins** (grapes)
    ray-ZIN

15) **cerise** (cherry)
    ce-ree-ZE

16) **pomme** (apple)
    POM

17) **poire** (pear)
    PWAR

18) **pamplemousse** (grapefruit)
    pam-pleh-MOOSE

19) **fruit du corossol** (soursop)
    frwee-du-coh-roh-SSOL

20) **noix de coco** (coconut)
    nwah-deuh-COCO

Je voudrais 1kg de poires.
I would like a kilo of pears.

Il mange un pamplemousse pour le petit-déjeuner.
He eats a grapefruit for breakfast.

J'adore la confiture de framboises.
I love raspberry jam.

LES LÉGUMES (VEGETABLES)

1) **chou-fleur** (cauliflower)
choo-FLEUR

2) **asperge** (asparagus)
ass-per-JE

3) **brocoli** (broccoli)
bro-coh-LEE

4) **chou** (cabbage)
CHOO

5) **artichaut** (artichoke)
art-tee-CHO

6) **chou de Bruxelles** (Brussels sprout)
choo-deuh-bru-SELLE

7) **maïs** (corn)
mah-EES

8) **laitue** (lettuce)
lay-TUE

9) **épinard** (spinach)
hay-pee-NAR

10) **tomate** (tomato)
toh-MAT

11) **concombre** (cucumber)
con-con-BREH

12) **courgette** (zucchini)
coor-JET

13) **champignon** (mushroom)
chan-pee-NYON

14) **roquette** (arugula)
roh-KET

15) **aubergine** (eggplant)
oh-ber-gee-NEH

16) **poivron** (bell pepper)
pwa-VRON

17) **oignon** (onion)
wah-NYON

18) **courge** (pumpkin/squash)
coor-JE

19) **pomme de terre** (potato)
pom-deuh-TER

20) **bette** (Swiss chard)
BET

J'ai préparé une soupe au chou.
I prepared a cabbage soup.

La salade de tomate manque de sauce.
The tomato salad lacks sauce.

Il y a des aubergines dans la moussaka.
There are eggplants in the Moussaka.

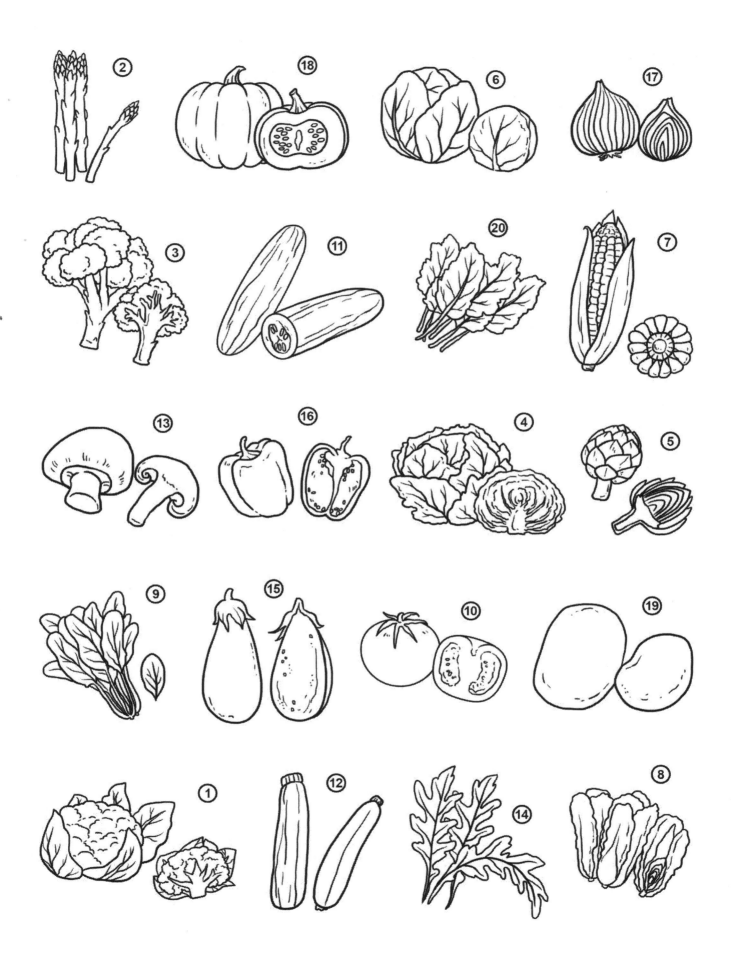

LES TECHNOLOGIES (TECHNOLOGY)

1) **portable** (mobile)
   por-tah-BLEH

2) **appareil** (device)
   ah-pah-RAYE

3) **ordinateur** (computer)
   or-dee-nah-TEUR

4) **webcam** (web cam)
   web-CAM

5) **clef USB** (flash drive)
   clay-U-S-BAY

6) **disque dur** (hard drive)
   disk-DUR

7) **carte mémoire** (memory card)
   kart-may-MWAR

8) **lecteur de carte** (card reader)
   lek-teur-deuh-KART

9) **sans fil (**wireless)
   san-FEEL

10) **panneau solaire** (solar panel)
    pah-no-soh-LAIR

11) **imprimante** (printer)
    im-pree-MANTE

12) **scanner** (scanner)
    ska-NAIR

J'ai un meeting via webcam.
I have a meeting via webcam.

La carte mémoire de mon appareil photo est pleine.
My camera's memory card is full.

Je vais enregistrer ces documents sur ma clef USB.
I am going to save these documents on my flash drive.

LES SCIENCES (SCIENCE)

1) **laboratoire** (laboratory)
   lah-boh-rah-TWAR

2) **chercheur** (researcher)
   chair-CHEUR

3) **calculs** (calculations)
   kal-CULE

4) **scientifique** (scientist)
   see-yan-tee-FEEK

5) **blouse de laboratoire** (lab coat)
   blooz-deuh-lah-boh-rah-TWAR

6) **expérience** (experiment)
   ex-pay-ree-YANCE

7) **équipement de protection** (personal protective equipment)
   hey-kip-man-deuh-pro-tec-see-YON

8) **test** (test)
   TEST

9) **prix** (prize)
   PREE

10) **risque** (risk)
    RISK

11) **instrument** (instrument)
    un-ss-tru-man

12) **statistiques** (statistics)
    stah-tees-TEEK

L'équipement de protection est obligatoire dans le laboratoire.
Personal protective equipment is mandatory in the laboratory.

Je suis venu faire un test COVID.
I have come for a COVID test.

Il travaille comme scientifique.
He works as a scientist.

L'ASTRONOMIE (ASTRONOMY)

1) **télescope** (telescope)
tay-lay-SCOPE

2) **Soleil** (sun)
soh-LAYE

3) **Lune** (moon)
LUN

4) **galaxie** (galaxy)
gah-lax-EE

5) **ceinture d'astéroïdes** (asteroid belt)
sin-TUR

6) **trou noir** (black hole)
troo-NWAR

7) **éclipse** (eclipse)
hey-CLIPS

8) **étoile filante** (shooting star)
hey-twal-fee-LANTE

9) **station spatiale** (space station)
sta-see-yon-spa-see-YAL

10) **naine blanche** (white dwarf)
nay-neh-blan-CHE

11) **géante rouge** (red giant)
jay-ante-roo-JE

12) **orbite** (orbit)
or-BEET

13) **constellation** (constellation)
cons-tel-ass-YON

14) **énergie noire** (dark energy)
hey-ner-gee-obs-CURE

15) **Pluton** (Pluto)
plu-TON

16) **Nébuleuse** (Nebula)
nay-bu-leuh-ZE

17) **Mercure** (Mercury)
mer-CURE

18) **Vénus** (Venus)
vay-nu-SS

19) **Terre** (Earth)
TER

20) **Mars** (Mars)
mar-SS

21) **Jupiter** (Jupiter)
ju-pee-TAIR

22) **Saturne** (Saturn)
sah-tur-NEH

23) **Uranus** (Uranus)
u-rah-NUS

24) **Neptune** (Neptune)
nep-tu-NEH

La nuit, tu peux voir toute la Galaxie.
At night, you can see the whole galaxy.

La station spatiale a atterri sur Mars.
The space station landed on Mars.

J'ai pris un coup de soleil.
I got a sunburn.

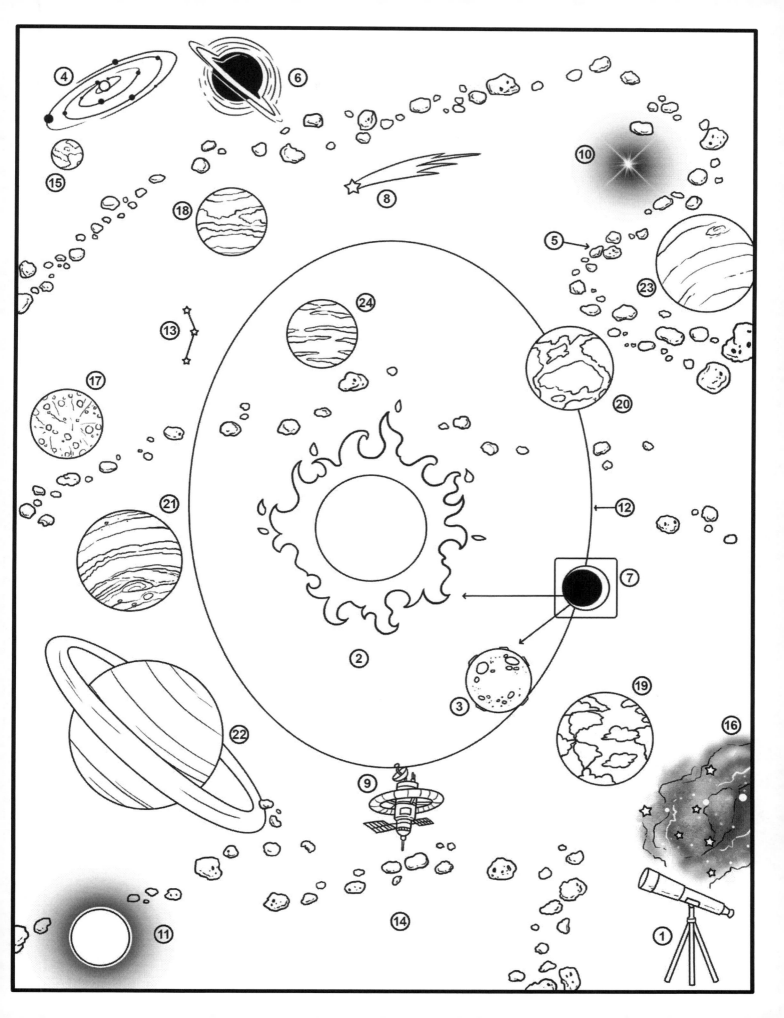

LA GÉOGRAPHIE (GEOGRAPHY)

1) **nord** (north)
NOR

2) **est** (east)
ess-TEH

3) **sud** (south)
SUD

4) **ouest** (west)
WEST

5) **Équateur** (Equator)
hay-kwa-TEUR

6) **tropique du Cancer** (Tropic of Cancer)
troh-peek-du-can-CER

7) **tropique du Capricorne** (Tropic of Capricorn)
troh-peek-du-ka-pree-CORN

8) **Pôle Sud** (South Pole)
pol-SUD

9) **Pôle Nord** (North Pole)
pol-NOR

10) **Cercle Arctique** (Arctic Circle)
ser-cleh-ar-TEEK

11) **continent** (continent)
con-tee-NENT

12) **outre-mer** (overseas)
ootre-MER

13) **Afrique** (Africa)
ah-FREAK

14) **Asie** (Asia)
ah-ZEE

15) **Amérique du Nord** (North America)
ah-may-reek-du-NOR

16) **Amérique Centrale** (Central America)
ah-may-reek-cen-TRAL

17) **Amérique du Sud** (South America)
ah-may-reek-du-SUD

18) **Europe** (Europe)
euh-ROP

19) **Océanie** (Oceania)
oh-say-ah-KNEE

20) **Antarctique** (Antarctica)
an-tar-TEEK

21) **méridien** (meridian)
may-ree-dee-YAN

22) **parallèle** (parallel)
par-ah-LEL

23) **océan Atlantique** (Atlantic Ocean)
oh-say-an-at-lan-TEEK

24) **océan Pacifique** (Pacific Ocean)
(oh-say-an-pah-see-FEEK

J'habite dans le sud de la France.
I live in the south of France.

J'adore surfer dans l'océan Atlantique.
I love to surf in the Atlantic Ocean.

Nous avons prévu un voyage en Europe.
We have planned a trip to Europe.

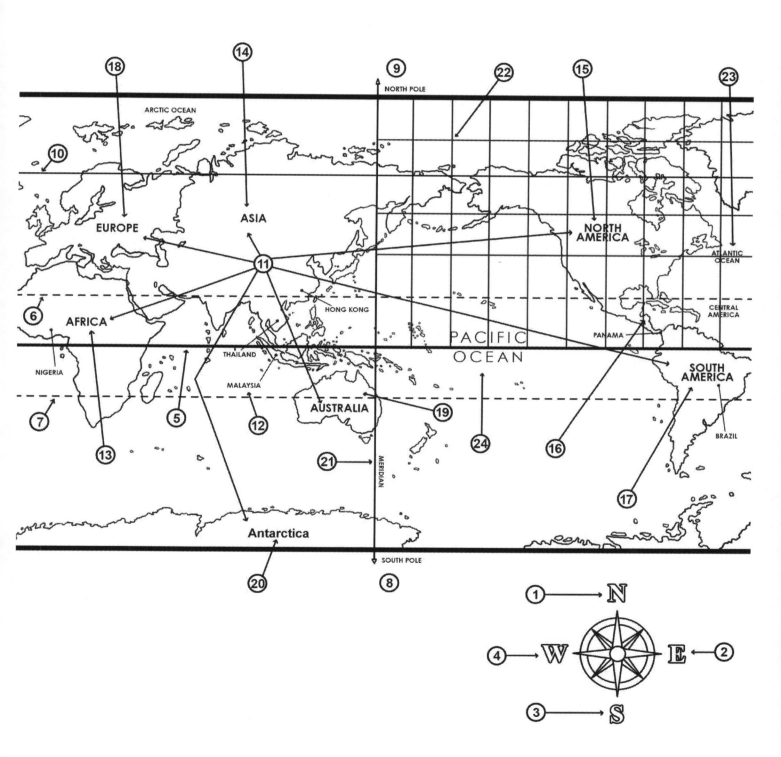

L'HÔPITAL (THE HOSPITAL)

1) **docteur** (doctor/medic)
doc-TEUR

2) **infirmière** (nurse)
un-feer-mee-YAIR

3) **ambulance** (ambulance)
am-bu-LANCE

4) **trousse de premier secours** (first-aid kit)
trouss-deuh-premier-seh-COUR

5) **thermomètre** (thermometer)
ter-moh-may-TREH

6) **civière** (stretcher)
see-vee-YAIR

7) **seringue** (syringe)
ser-un-GUE

8) **aiguille** (needle)
hay-gwee-YEH

9) **stéthoscope** (stethoscope)
stay-tos-COPE

10) **béquilles** (crutches)
bay-kee-YEH

11) **chaise roulante** (wheelchair)
chaiz-roo-LANTE

12) **observatoire** (observation room)
obs-hair-va-TWAR

13) **lit d'hôpital** (hospital bed)
lee-do-pee-TAL

14) **piqûre** (injection)
pee-KURE

15) **chirurgie** (surgery)
chee-rur-GEE

16) **antécédents médicaux** (medical history)
an-tay-say-dan-may-dee-COH

17) **patient** (patient)
pass-YIEN

18) **comprimé** (pill/tablet)
con-pree-MAY

J'ai un rendez-vous chez le docteur mercredi.
I have an appointment with the doctor on Wednesday.

Ce lit d'hôpital est très inconfortable.
This hospital bed is uncomfortable.

Ma fille veut devenir infirmière.
My daughter wants to become a nurse.

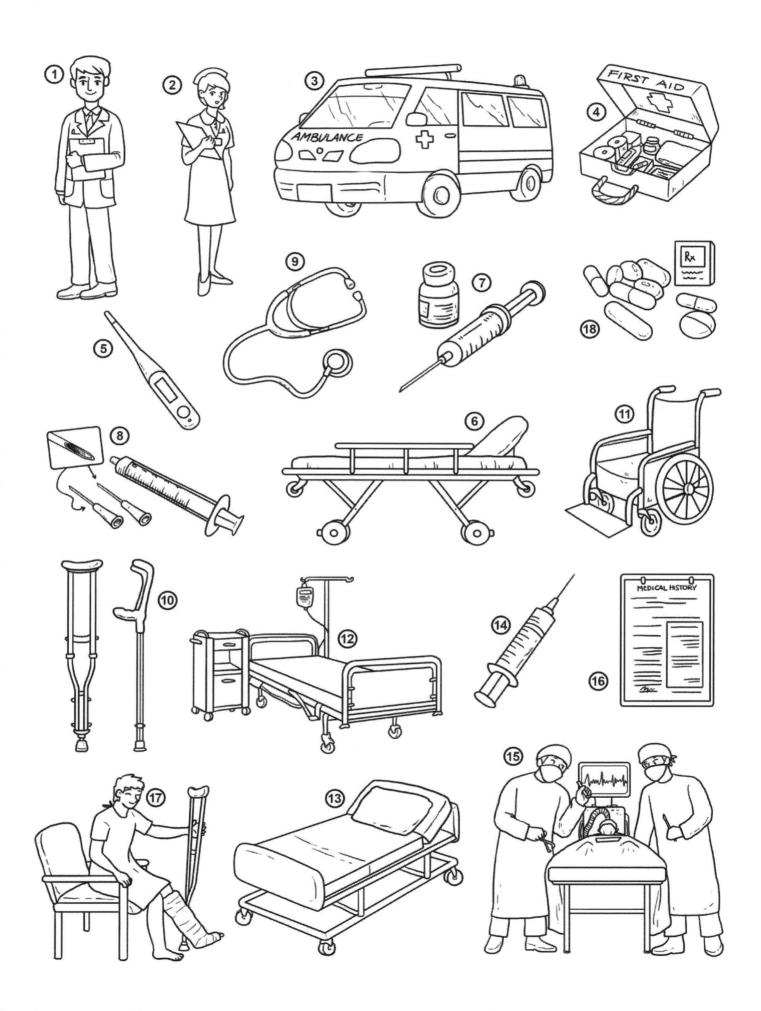

LA FERME (THE FARM)

1) **grange** (barn)
gran-JE

2) **écurie** (cowshed/stable)
hey-cu-REE

3) **fermier** (farmer)
fer-mee-YAY

4) **charrue** (plough)
cha-RUE

5) **silo** (silo)
see-LOH

6) **moulin** (mill)
mool-UN

7) **abreuvoir** (water trough)
ah-breuv-WAR

8) **poulailler** (henhouse)
poo-lah-YAY

9) **ruche** (beehive)
ru-SH

10) **botte de foin** (hay bale)
bot-deuh-FOOIN

11) **bétail** (cattle)
bay-TAILLE

12) **traire** (to milk)
tray-REH

13) **troupeau** (herd/flock)
troo-POH

14) **poule** (hen)
POOL

15) **puits** (well)
PWEE

16) **système d'irrigation** (irrigation system)
sis-tem-dee-ree-gah-see-YON

17) **épouvantail** (scarecrow)
hey-poo-van-TAYE

18) **chemin de campagne** (dirt road)
chem-un-deuh-camp-AGNE

Mes poules pondent une douzaine d'œufs par jour.
My hens lay a dozen eggs per day.

J'ai installé un épouvantail dans mon champ pour faire fuir les oiseaux.
I installed a scarecrow in my field to scare birds away.

Prenez à gauche et suivez le chemin de campagne.
Turn left and follow the dirt road.

QUIZ #5

Use arrows to match the corresponding translations:

a. laboratory

b. pear

c. drums

d. north

e. well

f. bagpipes

g. wheelchair

h. henhouse

i. eggplant

j. nurse

k. Earth

l. cauliflower

m. strawberry

n. flash drive

o. statistics

p. cherry

1. clé USB

2. chaise roulante

3. poire

4. chou-fleur

5. fraise

6. Terre

7. laboratoire

8. infirmière

9. cerise

10. statistiques

11. cornemuse

12. puit

13. nord

14. aubergine

15. batterie

16. poulailler

Fill in the blank spaces with the options below (use each word only once):

Mes grands-parents habitent en _____, à l'_____ de Copenhague. J'ai décidé de leur rendre visite le mois prochain. On ne se voit pas souvent car j'habite à New York, mais grâce à mon _____ et ma _____, nous restons en contact. Ma grand-mère est une excellente joueuse de _____. Elle avait l'habitude de jouer en concert dans des bars de la ville. C'est elle qui m'a appris à jouer de la _____ ! Mon grand-père est _____. Il fait pousser des _____ et des fruits. Il fait la meilleure tarte aux _____ et aux _____ du monde.

ordinateur	piano
choux de Bruxelles	pommes
Europe	fermier
guitare électrique	webcam
framboises	ouest

LA NOURRITURE (FOOD)

1) **raisin** (grape)
ray-z-UN

2) **noix** (walnuts)
NWAH

3) **viande** (meat)
vee-YANDE

4) **agneau** (lamb)
ah-NYO

5) **poisson** (fish)
pwa-ss-ON

6) **poulet** (chicken)
poo-LAY

7) **dinde** (turkey)
dun-DEH

8) **miel** (honey)
me-YEL

9) **sucre** (sugar)
su-CREH

10) **sel** (salt)
SEL

11) **poivre** (pepper)
pwa-VREH

12) **lard** (bacon)
LAR

13) **saucisses** (sausages)
so-see-SS

14) **sauce tomate** (ketchup)
soh-ss-toh-mah-TEH

15) **mayonnaise** (mayonnaise)
mah-yo-nay-ZEH

16) **moutarde** (mustard)
moo-TARDE

17) **confiture** (jam)
con-fee-TUR

18) **beurre** (butter)
beh-REH

19) **jus** (juice)
JU

20) **lait** (milk)
LAY

Je ne peux pas manger de frites sans mayonnaise.
I cannot eat fries without mayonnaise.

Les abeilles font du miel.
Bees make honey.

Tu préfères le poulet ou le poisson ?
Do you prefer chicken or fish?

LES PLATS (DISHES)

1) **lasagne** (lasagna)
lah-zah-GNEH

2) **omelette aux pommes de terre** (potato omelette)
om-lette-oh-pom-deuh-TER

3) **pain de viande** (meatloaf)
p-un-deuh-vee-YANDE

4) **nouilles sautées** (fried noodles)
noo-yeh-so-TAY

5) **macaroni au fromage** (macaroni and cheese)
mah-ka-ro-nee-oh-fro-mah-JE

6) **paëlla** (paella)
pah-hey-laLA

7) **travers de porc sauce barbecue** (barbecue ribs)
trah-ver-deuh-por-soss-barbe-CUE

8) **pain de maïs** (cornbread)
p-un-deuh-mah-EESS

9) **rouleau de printemps** (spring roll)
roo-loh-deuh-pr-un-TEM

10) **cheeseburger** (cheeseburger)
cheese-BURGER

11) **poulet frit** (fried chicken)
poo-ley-FREE

12) **salade César** (Caesar salad)
sah-lah-deh-say-ZAR

13) **soupe à l'oignon** (onion soup)
soop-ah-loh-NYON

14) **salade de chou** (coleslaw)
sah-lah-de-deuh-CHOO

15) **ailes de poulet épicées** (spicy chicken wings)
hay-leh-ron-deuh-poo-LAY

16) **cookies aux pépites de chocolat** (chocolate-chip cookies)
cookies-oh-pay-pit-deuh-cho-co-LAH

17) **tarte au citron vert** (key lime pie)
tart-oh-see-tron-VER

18) **cheesecake** (cheesecake)
cheese-CAKE

Les Américains adorent les macaronis au fromage.
Americans love macaroni and cheese.

Je vais commander la soupe à l'oignon.
I am going to order the onion soup.

Le cheesecake est mon dessert préféré.
Cheesecake is my favorite dessert.

LES FRUITS DE MER (SEAFOOD)

1) **anchois** (anchovy)
ansh-WAH

2) **morue** (cod)
moh-RUE

3) **araignée de mer** (spider crab)
ah-ray-gnyay-deuh-MER

4) **maquereau** (mackerel)
mah-keh-ROW

5) **homard** (lobster)
oh-MAR

6) **coquille St Jacques** (scallop)
coh-kee-yeh-ss-un-JACK

7) **vivaneau** (snapper)
vee-vah-NOH

8) **œufs de saumon** (salmon roe)
soh-MON

9) **crabe** (crab)
KRAB

10) **crustacés** (shellfish)
krus-tah-SAY

11) **anguille** (eel)
ahn-guee-YEH

12) **crevette** (shrimp)
kreh-VETTE

Je veux des anchois sur ma pizza.
I want anchovies on my pizza.

Les coquilles St Jacques sont très chères.
Scallops are very expensive.

J'ai acheté du saumon Ecossais pour le dîner.
I have bought Scottish salmon for dinner.

LES FORMES (SHAPES)

1) **cercle** (circle)
RON

2) **ovale** (oval)
oh-VAL

3) **triangle** (triangle)
tree-yan-GLEH

4) **rectangle** (rectangle)
rec-tan-GLEH

5) **carré** (square)
car-RAY

6) **trapèze** (trapezoid)
trah-pey-ZEH

7) **losange** (rhombus)
lo-ZANGE

8) **cube** (cube)
ku-BE

9) **pentagone** (pentagon)
p-un-tah-go-NEH

10) **hexagone** (hexagon)
X-ah-go-NEH

11) **flèche** (arrow)
FLESH

12) **croix** (cross)
CRWAH

13) **cœur** (heart)
KER

14) **étoile** (star)
hay-TWAL

15) **cylindre** (cylinder)
seal-un-DREH

16) **cône** (cone)
KOHNE

17) **pyramide** (pyramid)
pee-rah-mee-DEH

18) **sphère** (sphere)
ss-FAIR

19) **prisme** (prism)
pree-ss-MEH

Avez-vous visité la pyramide du Louvre ?
Have you visited the Louvre pyramid?

Mon bébé aime jouer avec des cubes.
My baby loves to play with cubes.

La route est barrée, il y a des cônes par terre.
The road is shut, there are cones on the floor.

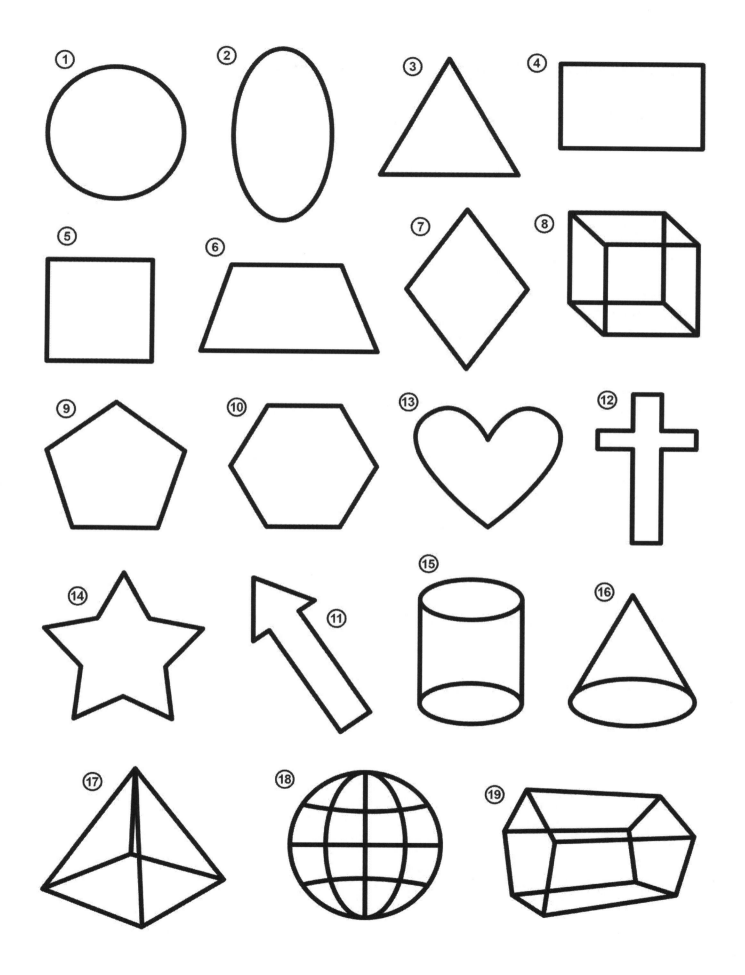

LE SUPERMARCHE (THE SUPERMARKET)

1) **chariot** (shopping cart)
   cha-ree-YO

2) **vitrine** (cabinet/display case)
   vee-tree-NEH

3) **client** (customer)
   clee-YAN

4) **caissier** (cashier)
   kayss-YAY

5) **reçu** (receipt)
   reh-SSUH

6) **boulangerie** (bakery)
   boo-lan-geh-REE

7) **fruits et légumes** (fruits and vegetables)
   frwee-hey-ley-GUM

8) **viande** (meat)
   vee-YANDE

9) **produits laitiers** (dairy products)
   pro-dwee-lay-TYAY

10) **poisson** (fish)
    pwa-SSON

11) **surgelés** (frozen food)
    sur-geh-LAY

12) **volaille** (poultry)
    vo-lah-YEH

13) **légumineuses** (legumes)
    lay-gu-mee-NEUZ

14) **snacks** (snacks)
    SNACKS

15) **desserts** (dessert)
    day-ss-HAIR

16) **boissons** (drinks)
    bwa-ss-ON

17) **articles ménagers** (household items)
    ar-tee-cleh-may-nah-JAY

18) **tapis roulant** (belt conveyor)
    tah-pee-roo-LAN

Je vais chercher mon pain à la boulangerie tous les matins.
I go get my bread at the bakery every morning.

Je suis végétarien, je ne mange pas de viande.
I am a vegetarian; I do not eat meat.

Ce magasin a une grande sélection de fruits et légumes.
This shop has a great selection of fruits and vegetables.

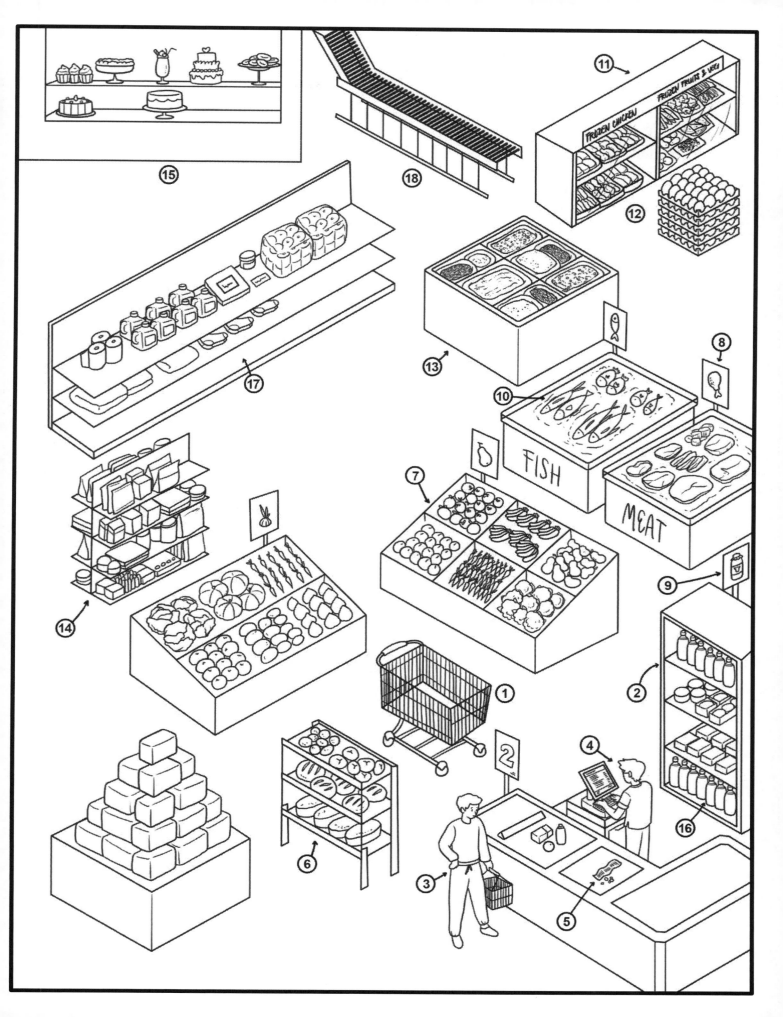

LES MEDIAS (MEDIA)

1) **magazine** (magazine)
mah-ga-ZINE

2) **fax** (fax)
FAX

3) **journal intime** (journal)
joor-nal-un-TEAM

4) **poste** (postal mail)
POST

5) **lettre** (letter)
lay-TREH

6) **radio** (radio)
rah-dee-YO

7) **bande dessinée** (comic)
band-dey-see-NAY

8) **livre** (book)
lee-VREH

9) **photographie** (photography)
pho-to-grah-FEE

10) **téléphone fixe** (landline phone)
tay-lay-phone-FIX

11) **télé** (TV)
tay-LAY

12) **films** (movies)
FILM

13) **téléphone portable** (mobile phone/cell phone)
tay-lay-phone-por-tah-BLEH

14) **langage des signes** (sign language)
lan-gage-day-see-GNEH

Le concert de Beyoncé passe à la télé demain soir.
Beyoncé's concert airs on TV tomorrow night.

Peux-tu me donner ton numéro de téléphone portable ?
Can you give me your cell number?

Je lui ai envoyé une lettre.
I have sent him a letter.

LE PARC D'ATTRACTIONS (THE FAIR/THE AMUSEMENT PARK)

1) **maison des miroirs** (house of mirrors)
   may-zon-day-mee-RWAR

2) **bateau pirate (**pirate ship/boat swing)
   bah-toh-pee-RAT

3) **guichet** (ticket booth)
   gee-CHAY

4) **balançoire** (swing ride)
   bah-lan-SSWAR

5) **montagne russe** (roller coaster)
   mon-tah-gneh-RUSS

6) **grande roue** (Ferris wheel)
   grand-ROO

7) **manège** (carousel/merry-go-round)
   mah-nay-GEH

8) **autos-tamponneuses** (bumper cars)
   oto-tam-poh-NEUZ

9) **tasses à thé** (teacups/cup and saucer)
   tass-ah-TAY

10) **pendule** (pendulum)
    pan-DUL

11) **salle d'arcade** (arcade room)
    sal-dar-KAHD

12) **corn dog** (corn dog)
    corn-DOG

13) **cône** (snow cone)
    coh-NEH

14) **barbe à papa** (cotton candy)
    barb-ah-PAPA

15) **pomme d'amour** (candy apple)
    pom-dah-MOOR

J'adore les montagnes russes.
I love roller coasters.

Il s'est perdu dans la maison des miroirs.
He got lost in the house of mirrors.

J'ai mangé trop de barbe à papa.
I ate too much cotton candy.

LES ÉVÉNEMENTS IMPORTANTS (LIFE EVENTS)

1) **naissance** (birth)
nay-ss-ANSSE

2) **baptême** (christening/baptism)
bat-EM

3) **premier jour d'école** (first day of school)
preh-mee-yay-joor-day-COL

4) **se faire des amis** (make friends)
seh-fair-day-zah-ME

5) **anniversaire** (birthday)
ah-knee-ver-SSAIR

6) **tomber amoureux** (fall in love)
tom-bay-ah-moo-REH

7) **remise des diplômes** (graduation)
reh-meez-deuh-dee-PLOME

8) **entrer à l'université** (to start university/begin college)
entray-ah-lu-nee-ver-see-TAY

9) **trouver un travail** (get a job)
troo-vay-un-trah-VAIL

10) **se mettre à son compte** (become an entrepreneur)
seh-metr-ah-son-con-TEH

11) **voyager à travers le monde** (travel around the world)
vwa-yah-jay-leuh-MOND

12) **se marier** (get married)
seh-mah-ree-YAY

13) **avoir un bébé** (have a baby)
av-war-un-bay-BAY

14) **célébrer un anniversaire** (celebrate a birthday)
say-lay-bray-un-ah-knee-ver-SSAIR

15) **retraite** (retirement)
reh-tray-TREH

16) **mort** (death)
MOR

Je vais me marier le mois prochain.
I am going to get married next month.

Mes parents sont à la retraite.
My parents are retired.

Gabrielle a enfin trouvé un travail.
Gabrielle has finally found a job.

LES ADJECTIFS I (ADJECTIVES I)

1) **gros** (big)
   GRO

2) **petit** (small)
   peh-TEE

3) **bruyant** (loud)
   brwee-YAN

4) **silencieux** (silent)
   see-lan-see-YEH

5) **long** (long)
   LON

6) **court** (short)
   COOR

7) **large** (wide)
   lar-GEH

8) **étroit** (narrow)
   hay-TRWAR

9) **cher** (expensive)
   CHAIR

10) **pas cher** (cheap)
    pah-CHAIR

11) **rapide** (fast)
    rah-PEED

12) **lent** (slow)
    LAN

13) **vide** (empty)
    VEED

14) **plein** (full)
    pl-UN

15) **doux** (soft)
    DOO

16) **dur** (hard)
    DUR

17) **grand** (tall)
    GRAN

18) **petit** (short)
    peh-TEE

Le chien du voisin est très bruyant.
The neighbor's dog is very loud.

Ce restaurant est bon et pas cher.
This restaurant is good and cheap.

Le guépard est l'animal le plus rapide.
The cheetah is the fastest animal.

QUIZ #6

Use arrows to match the corresponding translations:

a. book

b. dairy products

c. roller coaster

d. eel

e. circle

f. anchovy

g. jam

h. cotton candy

i. carousel

j. turkey

k. drinks

l. cross

m. nuts

n. fish

o. onion soup

p. arrow

1. boissons

2. anguille

3. noix

4. poisson

5. soupe à l'oignon

6. dinde

7. produits laitiers

8. croix

9. montagne russe

10. flèche

11. livre

12. confiture

13. barbe à papa

14. anchois

15. rond

16. manège

Fill in the blank spaces with the options below (use each word only once):

Pauline et ses amis ont organisé un délicieux repas après leur cérémonie de _____ le weekend dernier. En septembre, ils vont tous _____. Sauf Pauline, car elle veut d'abord _____, elle ira donc l'année prochaine. Le menu était très _____, mais le repas en valait le coup. C'était délicieux. En entrée, il y avait des _____ et du _____, Pauline était contente car elle adore les fruits de mer. Ensuite, il y avait le plat principal. Ils ont pu choisir entre les _____ et le _____ à la _____. Pauline a choisi le poulet mais malheureusement, il était un peu _____ et il manquait de _____. Pour le _____, ils se sont régalés avec un fondant au chocolat délicieux.

moutarde   dessert

cher   lasagnes

remise des diplômes   crabe

dur   poulet

sel   entrer à l'université

Coquilles St Jacques   Voyager à travers le monde

139

LES ADJECTIFS II (ADJECTIVES II)

1) **nouveau** (new)
   noo-VOH

2) **vieux** (old)
   vee-YEUH

3) **confortable** (comfortable)
   con-for-tah-BLEH

4) **inconfortable** (uncomfortable)
   un-con-for-tah-BLEH

5) **dangereux** (dangerous)
   gan-geh-REH

6) **irritant** (annoying)
   ee-ree-TAN

7) **fragile** (shaky)
   frah-GEEL

8) **complet** (complete)
   con-PLAY

9) **incomplet** (incomplete)
   un-con-PLAY

10) **cassé** (broken)
    kah-SSAY

11) **superbe** (gorgeous)
    su-PERB

12) **vertueux** (virtuous)
    ver-tu-EUH

13) **similaire** (similar)
    see-mee-LAIR

14) **différent** (different)
    dee-fay-RAN

15) **ouvert** (open)
    oo-VER

16) **fermé** (closed)
    fer-MAY

Ces jumeaux sont très similaires.
Those twins are very similar.

Mon canapé est vieux mais confortable.
My sofa is old but comfortable.

Ce magasin n'est jamais ouvert !
This shop is never open!

LES ADVERBES (ADVERBS)

1) **ici** (here)
ee-SEE

2) **là-bas** (there)
lah-BAH

3) **près de** (near)
pray-DEUH

4) **loin** (far)
loo-UN

5) **en haut** (up)
an-OH

6) **en bas** (down)
an-BAH

7) **dans** (inside)
DAN

8) **dehors** (outside)
deuh-OR

9) **devant** (ahead)
deuh-VAN

10) **derrière** (behind)
der-YER

11) **non** (no)
NON

12) **oui** (yes)
WEE

13) **maintenant** (now)
mun-teh-NAN

14) **bien** (well/good/right)
bee-YIN

15) **mal** (bad/wrong)
MAL

Je t'attends en bas.
I am waiting for you downstairs.

Appelle-moi maintenant.
Call me now.

On mange ici ou là-bas ?
Are we eating here or over there?

LES DIRECTIONS (DIRECTIONS)

1) **bloc** (block)
   BLOC

2) **place** (square)
   PLASS

3) **parc** (park)
   PARK

4) **métro** (subway)
   may-TRO

5) **coin** (corner)
   c-WUN

6) **avenue** (avenue)
   ah-veh-NU

7) **rue** (street)
   RU

8) **arrêt de bus** (bus stop)
   a-ray-deuh-BUS

9) **feux** (traffic lights)
   FEUH

10) **passage piéton** (crossing/crosswalk)
    pah-ssaje-piay-TON

11) **en haut** (up)
    en-OH

12) **en bas** (down)
    en-BAH

13) **gauche** (left)
    GOSH

14) **droite** (right)
    DRWAT

15) **panneaux** (road signs)
    pah-NO

16) **police de circulation** (traffic police)
    poh-lees-deuh-seer-cu-lah-SSION

Je n'aime pas l'odeur du métro.
I do not like the smell of the subway.

Prenez la seconde rue à gauche.
Take the second street on the left.

Vous devez emprunter le passage piéton.
You must use the crosswalk.

LE RESTAURANT (THE RESTAURANT)

1) **gérant** (manager)
   jay-RAN

2) **table** (table)
   tah-BLEH

3) **menu** (menu)
   meh-NU

4) **plat** (dish)
   PLAH

5) **apéritif** (appetizer)
   ah-pay-ree-TEEF

6) **entrée** (starter)
   an-TRAY

7) **plat principal** (main course)
   plah-prun-see-PAL

8) **dessert** (dessert)
   day-SSER

9) **dîner** (diner)
   dee-NAY

10) **chef** (cook)
    CHEF

11) **serveur** (waiter)
    ser-VEUR

12) **serveuse** (waitress)
    ser-VEUZ

13) **pourboire** (tip)
    poor-BWAR

14) **chaise haute** (high chair)
    chaiz-ho-I

15) **carte des vins** (wine list)
    kart-dey-VIN

16) **chef pâtissier** (pastry chef)
    chaf-pah-tee-SSYAY

Voulez-vous voir notre menu ?
Would you like to see our menu?

Je vais prendre un apéritif s'il-vous-plaît.
I will have an appetizer please.

Veuillez féliciter votre chef !
Congratulate your chef!

LE CENTRE COMMERCIAL (THE MALL)

1) **étage** (floor)
hay-tah-GEH

2) **aquarium** (aquarium)
ah-qwa-ree-YUM

3) **aire de restauration** (food court)
air-deuh-ress-toh-rah-SSION

4) **ascenseur** (elevator)
ass-en-SEUR

5) **escalator** (escalators)
ess-kah-lah-TEUR

6) **sortie de secours** (emergency exit)
sor-tee-deuh-seh-COUR

7) **salon de beauté** (beauty salon)
sah-lon-deug-boh-TAY

8) **magasin de vêtements** (clothing store)
mah-gah-zun-deuh-vet-MAN

9) **aire de jeux** (playground)
air-deuh-JE

10) **garde de sécurité** (security guard)
gard-deuh-say-cu-ree-TAY

11) **caméra de surveillance** (surveillance camera)
kah-may-rah-deuh-sur-vey-YANCE

12) **boulangerie** (bakery)
boo-lan-geh-REE

13) **magasin de sport** (sports store)
mah-ga-zin-deuh-SPORT

14) **fontaine** (fountain)
fon-TAINE

Prenez l'ascenseur et arrêtez-vous au deuxième étage.
Take the elevator and stop on the second floor.

Je vais emmener mon fils à l'air de jeux.
I am going to take my son to the playground.

J'habite à côté du magasin de sport.
I live next to the sports store.

LES VERBES I (VERBS I)

1) **parler** (to talk)
   pay-LAY

2) **boire** (to drink)
   BWAR

3) **manger** (to eat)
   man-JAY

4) **marcher** (to walk)
   mar-CHAY

5) **ouvrir** (to open)
   oo-VREER

6) **fermer** (to close)
   fer-MAY

7) **donner** (to give)
   don-NAY

8) **voir** (to see)
   v-WAR

9) **suivre** (to follow)
   swee-VREH

10) **câliner** (to hug)
    cah-lee-NAY

11) **embrasser** (to kiss)
    em-brah-SAY

12) **acheter** (to buy)
    ah-che-TAY

13) **écouter** (to listen)
    hay-coo-TAY

14) **chanter** (to sing)
    chan-TAY

15) **danser** (to dance)
    dan-SAY

Vous devez fermer la fenêtre.
You must close the window.

Suivez- moi !
Follow me!

Je lui ai donné 10 euros.
I gave him 10 euros.

LES VERBES II (VERBS II)

1) **écrire** (to write)
   hay-KRIR

2) **lire** (to read)
   LEER

3) **nettoyer** (to clean)
   ney-twa-YAY

4) **récupérer** (to pick up)
   ray-cu-pay-RAY

5) **trouver** (to find)
   troo-VAY

6) **laver** (to wash)
   lah-VAY

7) **regarder** (to watch)
   reh-gar-DAY

8) **réparer** (to fix)
   ray-par-HAY

9) **penser** (to think)
   pen-SAY

10) **prendre** (to take)
    pren-DREH

11) **couper** (to cut)
    coo-PAY

12) **arrêter** (to stop)
    ar-ray-TAY

13) **pleurer** (to cry)
    pleh-RAY

14) **sourire** (to smile)
    soo-REER

15) **aider** (to help)
    ai-DAY

Arrête de pleurer.
Stop crying.

Je vais nettoyer mon appartement.
I am going to clean my flat.

J'ai réparé le moteur de ma voiture.
I have repaired my car's engine.

CONSTRUCTION I (CONSTRUCTION I)

1) **grue** (crane)
GRU

2) **ruban rouge et blanc** (hazard tape)
ru-ban-roo-JE

3) **cône de signalisation** (traffic cone)
kohn-deuh-see-nya-lee-za-SSION

4) **pelleteuse** (construction shovel)
pel-teuh-ZE

5) **marteau** (hammer)
mar-TOW

6) **pince coupante** (wire cutters)
pin-sse-coo-pan-TEH

7) **rouleau à peinture** (paint roller)
roo-loh-ah-pin-TUR

8) **tronçonneuse** (chainsaw)
trons-oh-NEUZ

9) **perceuse** (drill)
per-SSEUZ

10) **marteau-piqueur** (jackhammer)
mar-tow-pee-KER

11) **pinces** (pliers)
pin-SS

12) **tournevis** (screwdriver)
toor-neuh-VISS

La tronçonneuse fait trop de bruit.
The chainsaw is too loud.

Il me faut un marteau pour accrocher ce tableau.
I need a hammer to hang this picture.

Donne-moi le tournevis.
Give me the screwdriver.

CONSTRUCTION II (CONSTRUCTION II)

1) **boîte à outils** (toolbox)
bwat-ah-oo-TEE

2) **casque de sécurité** (work helmet/hard hat)
cask-deuh-say-cu-ree-TAY

3) **plan** (blueprint)
PLAN

4) **tuyaux** (pipes)
twee-YO

5) **truelle** (trowel)
tru-EL

6) **bétonnière** (concrete mixer)
bay-toh-NIERE

7) **brique** (brick)
BRIK

8) **matériaux de construction** (building materials)
mah-tay-ree-yo-deuh-cons-truc-SSION

9) **carreaux** (tiles)
kah-ROH

10) **ciment** (cement)
see-MAN

11) **sable** (sand)
sah-BLEH

12) **graviers** (gravel)
grah-vee-YAY

Les maisons anglaises sont en brique.
English houses are made of bricks.

Ma boîte à outils est dans le garage.
My toolbox is in the garage.

Nous avons mis du gravier dans notre allée.
We have put gravel down in our front yard.

QUIZ #7

Use arrows to match the corresponding translations:

a. waitress   1. parler

b. left   2. ouvert

c. old   3. loin

d. bus stop   4. chanter

e. bad   5. droite

f. playground   6. aire de jeux

g. right   7. ascenseur

h. to talk   8. boulangerie

i. main course   9. fermé

j. closed   10. acheter

k. to sing   11. gauche

l. elevator   12. mal

m. to buy   13. vieux

n. open   14. serveuse

o. bakery   15. arrêt de bus

p. far   16. plat principal

Fill in the blank spaces with the options below (use each word only once):

Voici les directions pour vous rendre au _____, depuis la place de la _____. Il faut _____ la première rue à _____ et aller jusqu'aux _____. Une fois que le feu est vert, tournez à gauche. _____ l'église, il y a une station de _____. Passez la station et il faudra encore _____ pendant 10 minutes. Vous verrez le magasin sur votre gauche.

feux	magasin de vêtements
marcher	droite
Fontaine	prendre
derrière	métro

LES PLANTES ET ARBRES (PLANTS AND TREES)

1) **fleurs sauvages** (wildflower)
fleur-so-VAJ

2) **herbe** (herb)
HERB

3) **champignon** (mushroom)
cham-pee-NION

4) **mauvaise herbe** (weed)
moh-vaiz-HERB

5) **algue** (seaweed)
ALG

6) **fougère** (fern)
foo-JAIR

7) **roseau** (reed)
roh-ZO

8) **bambou** (bamboo)
bam-BOO

9) **lierre** (ivy)
lee-YAIR

10) **mousse** (moss)
MOOSS

11) **herbe** (grass)
HERB

12) **palmier** (palm tree)
pal-mee-YAY

13) **mangrove** (mangrove)
man-GROV

14) **cactus** (cactus)
kak-TUS

Il m'a offert un bouquet de fleurs sauvages.
He gifted me a bouquet of wildflowers.

Le bambou pousse très vite.
Bamboo grows very fast.

Ce soir nous mangeons des pâtes aux champignons.
Tonight, we are eating mushroom pasta.

LE CARNAVAL (THE CARNIVAL)

1) **masque** (mask)
   MASK

2) **déguisement** (costume/disguise)
   day-geez-MAN

3) **char** (float)
   CHAR

4) **fleurs** (flowers)
   FLEUR

5) **caisse claire** (snare drum)
   kaiss-KLAIR

6) **clown** (clown)
   CLOWN

7) **super-héros** (superhero)
   su-pair-hay-ROH

8) **princesse** (princess)
   prin-CESS

9) **astronaute** (astronaut)
   ass-troh-NAUT

10) **mime** (mime)
    MEEM

11) **prisonnier** (prisoner)
    pree-zoh-NIAY

12) **appareil ménager** (household appliance)
    ah-pah-raiy-may-nah-JAY

13) **fée** (fairy)
    FEY

14) **bûcheron** (lumberjack)
    bu-che-RON

Je lis un conte de fées à ma fille chaque soir.
I read a fairy tale to my daughter every evening.

Vous devez porter un masque dans l'hôpital.
You must wear a mask in the hospital.

Diana était la princesse du peuple.
Diana was the people's princess.

L'ATELIER (THE WORKSHOP)

1) **outil** (tool)
   oo-TEE

2) **sellerie** (saddlery)
   sel-REE

3) **menuiserie** (carpentry/woodwork)
   meh-nwee-ZREE

4) **tapisserie** (upholstery/tapestry)
   tah-pee-ss-REE

5) **cordonnerie** (shoemaking/shoerepair)
   kor-don-REE

6) **orfèvrerie** (silversmith)
   or-fev-REE

7) **forgeron** (blacksmith)
   for-je-RON

8) **mécanicien** (mechanic)
   may-kah-nee-SSIEN

9) **textile** (textile)
   tex-TEEL

10) **boulangerie** (bakery)
    boo-lan-geh-REE

11) **bijou fantaisie** (costume jewelry)
    bijoo-deuh-fan-tay-ZEE

12) **chaussures** (footwear)
    cho-SSUR

13) **maintenance** (maintenance)
    mun-teh-NANS

14) **réparation** (repair)
    ray-pah-rah-see-YON

15) **peinture** (painting)
    pin-TUR

16) **pâtisserie** (pastry)
    pah-tIseh-REE

Le mécanicien a fini de réparer ma voiture.
The mechanic has finished repairing my car.

Je suis l'agent de maintenance.
I am the maintenance guy.

Je voudrais acheter votre peinture.
I would like to buy your painting.

L'ÉPICERIE (THE GROCERY STORE)

1) **pâtes** (pasta)
PAT

2) **riz** (rice)
REE

3) **avoine** (oat)
ah-VWAN

4) **pain** (bread)
p-UN

5) **huiles** (oils)
HWEEL

6) **sauces** (sauces)
SAUSS

7) **vinaigrette** (salad dressings)
sauss-deuh-SALAD

8) **condiments** (condiments)
con-dee-MAN

9) **conserves** (canned goods)
con-SERV

10) **jambon** (ham)
jam-BON

11) **fromage** (cheese)
froh-mah-JE

12) **beurre de cacahuètes** (peanut butter)
beur-deuh-kaka-UETTE

13) **bonbon** (candy)
bon-BON

14) **haricots** (beans)
ah-ree-COH

15) **café** (coffee)
ca-FAY

16) **thé** (tea)
TÉ

Je veux manger un sandwich au beurre de cacahuètes.
I want to eat a peanut butter sandwich.

Je prends du lait d'avoine dans mon café.
I take oat milk in my coffee.

On trouve les meilleurs fromages du monde en France.
You can find the best cheeses in the world in France.

VOYAGE I (TRAVEL AND LIVING I)

1) **hôte** (host)
   oh-TEH

2) **touriste** (tourist)
   too-RIST

3) **voyageur** (traveler)
   vwa-yah-JEUR

4) **bagage** (luggage)
   bah-GAGE

5) **bagage à main** (hand luggage)
   bah-gage-ah-MUN

6) **appareil photo** (camera)
   ah-pah-reil-FOTO

7) **hôtel** (hotel)
   oh-TEL

8) **auberge** (hostal)
   og-BERJE

9) **chambre d'hôte** (Bed & Breakfast/inn)
   cham-breh-doh-TEH

10) **cabane** (cabin)
    kah-BANE

11) **tente** (tent)
    TANT

12) **vol** (flight)
    VOL

13) **départ** (departure)
    day-PAR

14) **arrivée** (arrival)
    ar-ee-VAY

J'ai réservé une chambre d'hôte pour trois nuits.
I booked a bed and breakfast for three nights.

Le départ du vol est à 13h30.
The flight departs at 1.30 p.m.

N'oublie pas l'appareil photo!
Do not forget the camera!

VOYAGE II (TRAVEL AND LIVING II)

1) **ville** (town)
VEEL

2) **carte** (map)
KART

3) **arrêt de bus** (bus stop)
array-deuh-BUS

4) **taxi** (taxi)
TAXI

5) **location de voiture** (car rental)
loh-cah-see-yon-deuh-vwa-TUR

6) **gare** (train station)
GAR

7) **aéroport** (airport)
ah-hey-roh-POR

8) **passeport** (passport)
pass-POR

9) **carte d'identité** (ID/identification card)
kart-dee-den-tee-TAY

10) **monnaie** (currency)
moh-NAY

11) **liquide** (cash)
lee-KID

12) **carte bancaire** (debit card)
kart-ban-KAIR

13) **carte de crédit** (credit card)
kart-deuh-cray-DEE

14) **guide touristique** (tourist guide)
geed-too-rees-TEEK

Je dois renouveler mon passeport.
I must renew my passport.

Vous payez par carte bancaire ou en liquide ?
Are you paying by debit card or cash?

Pouvez-vous me réserver un taxi ?
Could you book a taxi for me?

LES JOUETS (TOYS)

1) **balle** (ball)
   BAL

2) **ours en peluche** (teddy bear)
   oors-an-peh-LUCHE

3) **train** (train)
   tr-UN

4) **skateboard** (skateboard)
   skate-BOARD

5) **poupée** (doll)
   poo-PAY

6) **voiture de course** (race car)
   coursse-deuh-vwa-TUR

7) **robot** (robot)
   roh-BOH

8) **cerf volant** (kite)
   ser-voh-LAN

9) **batterie** (drum)
   bah-TREE

10) **cerceau** (hula hoop)
    ser-SO

11) **wagon** (wagon)
    va-GON

12) **blocs** (blocks)
    BLOK

13) **xylophone** (xylophone)
    xee-loh-PHONE

14) **camion** (truck)
    kah-mee-YON

15) **avion** (airplane)
    ah-vee-YON

16) **briques** (bricks)
    BRIK

J'ai appris à jouer de la batterie il y a 10 ans.
I learned to play the drums 10 years ago.

Ma fille a perdu son ours en peluche.
My daughter has lost her teddy bear.

Lance-moi la balle !
Throw me the ball!

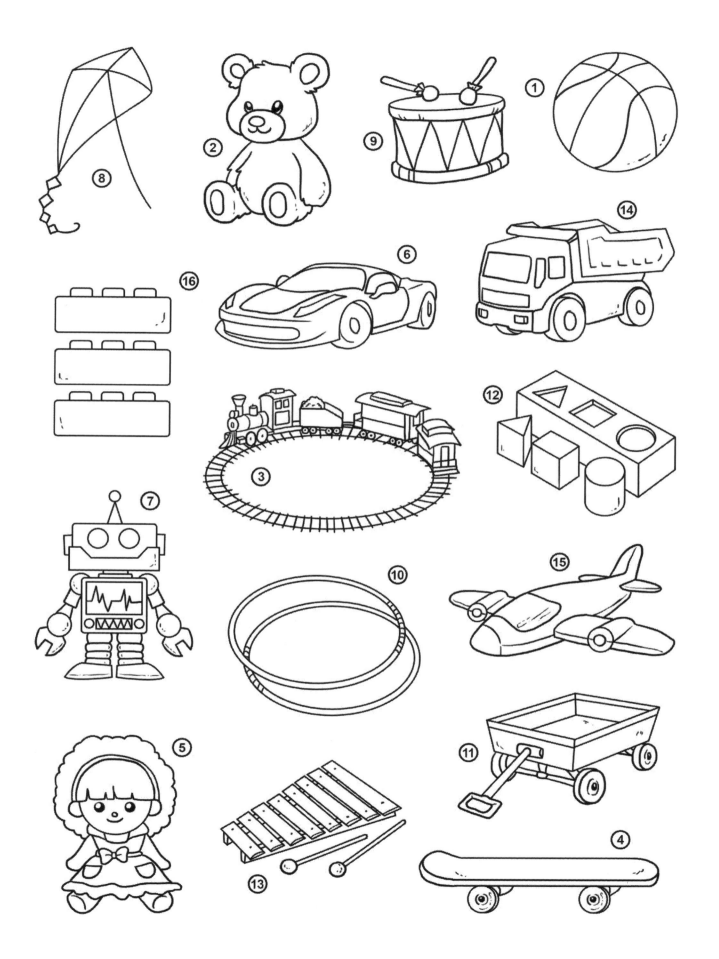

LA FÊTE D'ANNIVERSAIRE (THE BIRTHDAY PARTY)

1) **banderole d'anniversaire** (birthday banner)
ban-deuh-rol-dah-nee-ver-SAIR

2) **décoration** (decoration)
day-co-rah-see-YON

3) **cadeau** (present/gift)
kah-DO

4) **vaisselle** (tableware)
vay-SEL

5) **personne qui fête son anniversaire** (birthday person)
per-sonne-ki-fett-son-ah-nee-ver-SAIR

6) **ballon** (balloon)
bah-LON

7) **gâteau d'anniversaire** (birthday cake)
gah-to-dah-nee-ver-SAIR

8) **assiettes** (plates)
ass-YETTE

9) **fourchettes** (forks)
foor-CHETTE

10) **cuillères** (spoons)
cwee-YIER

11) **verres** (cups)
VER

12) **paille** (straw)
pah-YEH

13) **piñata** (piñata)
pee-nya-TA

14) **bougie** (candle)
boo-JEE

15) **chapeau** (hat)
chah-PO

16) **invités** (guests)
un-vee-TAY

J'ai reçu beaucoup de cadeaux pour mon anniversaire.
I received a lot of gifts for my birthday.

Les invités sont tous partis.
All the guests have left.

Elle m'a fabriqué une arche de ballons.
She made me a balloon arch.

LES OPPOSÉS (OPPOSITES)

1) **propre** (clean)
   pro-PREH

2) **sale** (dirty)
   SAL

3) **peu** (few)
   PEH

4) **beaucoup** (many)
   boh-COO

5) **attaque** (attack)
   ATTAK

6) **défense** (defense)
   day-FENSE

7) **droit** (straight)
   DRWA

8) **courbé** (curved)
   koor-BAY

9) **ensemble** (together)
   an-san-BLEH

10) **séparé** (separated)
    say-pah-RAY

11) **jeune** (young)
    JEUN

12) **vieux** (old)
    vee-YEUH

13) **richesse** (wealth)
    ree-CHESS

14) **pénurie** (shortage)
    pay-nu-REE

15) **concave** (concave)
    con-KAHV

16) **convexe** (convex)
    con-VEX

Mes parents sont séparés.
My parents are separated.

Je suis la plus jeune.
I am the youngest.

Cette assiette est sale.
This plate is dirty.

QUIZ #8

Use arrows to match the corresponding translations:

a. arrival

b. cheese

c. teddy bear

d. tourist guide

e. map

f. forks

g. grass

h. candle

i. doll

j. airport

k. truck

l. flowers

m. tent

n. mask

o. rice

p. candy

1. tente

2. poupée

3. fleurs

4. camion

5. masque

6. fromage

7. bonbon

8. aéroport

9. riz

10. herbe

11. ours en peluche

12. carte

13. arrivée

14. bougie

15. guide touristique

16. fourchettes

Fill in the blank spaces with the options below (use each word only once):

Ma cousine Coline est venue me rendre visite pour mon anniversaire. Son voyage était un vrai cauchemar ! Pour commencer, elle a manqué le _____ pour l'amener à l'_____. Elle a presque raté son _____. En descendant de l'avion, elle s'est rendu compte qu'elle avait laissé son _____ à l'aéroport, qui contenait son portefeuille avec son _____ et sa _____. Une fois arrivée en _____, il y avait tellement de _____ que toutes les rues étaient bloquées par des embouteillages. Elle voulait s'arrêter pour acheter un _____ mais elle n'a pas pu trouver de boulangerie car elle avait aussi perdu son _____. Elle n'avait pas non plus de cadeau, donc elle s'est arrêtée dans le seul magasin ouvert, qui était un magasin de jouets, et elle a acheté un _____ vraiment mignon.

touristes	gâteau d'anniversaire
carte d'identité	départ
ville	guide touristique
aéroport	bagage à main
passeport	ours en peluche
vol	taxi

CONCLUSION

While there is certainly much more to say about the French language, we hope that this general overview help will you to understand and use the words and phrases in this dictionary, as well as your own words and phrases, as you continue your journey to bilingualism.

We would like to leave you with a few suggestions for a pleasant and fruitful language learning experience:

1. Learn what you need and what you love.

   While survival French is indispensable, mechanical memorization of long lists of words is not the best use of your time and energy. Make sure to focus on the vocabulary that is important and useful to you in your life. Perhaps you need French for work, or to visit family and friends. In this case, make sure that you focus on the vocabulary that will be useful to reach these goals.

2. Do not skip learning grammar and tenses. Although it is not the most exciting part of learning a language, spending some time perfecting your grammar is the key to being able to manipulate the language in the long term.

3. Use available media to practice all aspects of the language. Movies, music, and social media. provide the opportunity to practice reading, writing, and listening at any time from your phone or your computer. Aim to spend 20 minutes a day on your practice of the French language in order to make good progress.

4. Practice speaking as soon as you can with a native speaker. You can join speaking groups in real life or online.

5. Remember: **Communication before perfection**. It takes years to master a language, and fluency is not achieved easily. It requires commitment and regular practice. However, if you get to visit a French speaking country, do not hesitate to try to speak French to everyone you meet. This will give you the motivation and the confidence to carry on learning. You might feel scared at first but do not worry, people will be kind to you!

6. Enjoy the journey!

ANSWERS

QUIZ #1

A-13. B-11. c-10. D-15. e-9. f-12. g-6. h-14. i-8. j-1. k-5. l-2.
m-16. n-7. o-4. p-3.

Ma **mère** et mon père ne sont plus ensemble depuis des années. Tout le monde est toujours **surpris** de voir à quel point ils s'entendent bien pour un **couple divorcé**. Ma **sœur** est ma meilleure amie. Elle est d'une grande **gentillesse**, elle a un **cœur** d'or. Quant à moi, je suis **sérieux** et tout le monde dit que j'ai beaucoup de **courage**. J'adore les animaux, surtout les **chiens**. Demain soir, nous sommes invités chez mon père pour dîner. Je crois qu'il va préparer une **dinde**. J'espère que je me sentirai mieux d'ici là car aujourd'hui, j'ai très mal à la **tête** et j'ai le nez **bouché**.

QUIZ # 2

A-10. b-5. C-8. d-9. e-2. f-13. g-15. h-16. i-3. J-12. k-1. l-4.
m-6. n-7. o-11. p-14.

Phil est professeur de maternelle. La semaine dernière, il a amené la classe visiter une ferme. La météo avait annoncé de la pluie, mais il a fait très **chaud**. C'était une journée très **ensoleillée**. Phil avait mis un **jeans**, des **chaussures** de marche et un gros **manteau**. Malheureusement, il s'est senti inconfortable toute la journée. Pendant la visite de la ferme, les enfants ont vu des cochons, des chevaux et des **vaches**. Il y avait aussi une ruche avec des centaines d'**abeilles**. Par contre, il y avait aussi des **guêpes** et l'une d'elle a piqué Phil !

QUIZ # 3

a-16. B-14. C-9. D-8. e-7. F-11. G-3. h-5. i-13. J-12. K-4. l-2.
m-1. n-15. o-6 p-10.

L'automne, c'est ma saison préférée. Chaque année, j'attends octobre avec impatience pour **décorer le jardin** et aussi mon **balcon**. Ma famille et moi aimons **creuser des citrouilles** et les placer dans toute la maison. J'en mets toujours une devant la **cheminée**, elles ressemblent à de petites **lampes** effrayantes ! Le 31 octobre, c'est Halloween. Nous allons chercher des bonbons chez les voisins. Après ça, vers **minuit**, nous allumons des **bougies épicées**, et nous nous relaxons dans le **canapé** en buvant un bon **chocolat chaud**. En général, mon frère joue à la **console de jeux vidéo**. En novembre, c'est le moment de faire du **ski** et de visiter la **patinoire** de notre ville. J'adore ça !

QUIZ # 4

a-15.   b-7.   c-9.   d-13.   e-11.   f-10.   G-12.   H-14.   i-8.   J-2.   K-1.   l-16.
m-4.   n-5.   o-6.   p-3.

Gérald est **étudiant** en ingénierie civile à l'université de Nantes. Il est en troisième année. Plus tard, il veut devenir **ingénieur** ou **homme d'affaires**. Son but, c'est de devenir riche et de voyager à travers le monde. Il rêve de jouer au **volley** sur une **plage** des Caraïbes, d'acheter son propre **bateau** ou bien de faire du **jet ski** sur la mer. Son **professeur** favori, c'est Mr Rendal. Il est très intelligent et charismatique. Gérald espère lui ressembler plus tard. Mais pour le moment, il doit se rendre à la laverie pour utiliser **la machine à laver** et laver son **linge sale**. Avant cela, il doit aller au supermarché pour acheter de la **lessive** et de l'**assouplissant** car il n'en a plus.

QUIZ # 5

a-7.   b-3.   c-15   d-13.   e-12.   f-11.   g-2.   h-16.   i-14.   j-8.   k-6.   l-4.
m-5.   n-1.   o-10.   p-9.

Mes grands-parents habitent en **Europe**, à l'**ouest** de Copenhague. J'ai décidé de leur rendre visite le mois prochain. On ne se voit pas souvent car j'habite à New York, mais grâce à mon **ordinateur** et ma **webcam**, nous restons en contact. Ma grand-mère est une excellente joueuse de **piano**. Elle avait l'habitude de jouer en concert dans des bars de la ville. C'est elle qui m'a appris à jouer de la **guitare électrique !** Mon grand-père est **fermier**. Il fait pousser des **choux de Bruxelles** et des fruits. Il fait la meilleure tarte aux **pommes** et aux **framboises** du monde.

QUIZ # 6

a-11.   b-7.   c-9.   d-2.   e-15.   f-14.   g-12.   h-13.   i-16.   j-6.   k-1.   l-8.
m-3.   n-4.   o-5.   p-10.

Pauline et ses amis ont organisé un délicieux repas après leur cérémonie de **remise des diplômes** le weekend dernier. En septembre, ils vont tous **entrer à l'université**. Sauf Pauline, car elle veut d'abord **voyager à travers le monde**, elle ira donc l'année prochaine. Le menu était très **cher**, mais le repas en valait le coup. C'était délicieux. En entrée, il y avait des **coquilles St Jacques** et du **crabe,** Pauline était contente car elle adore les fruits de mer. Ensuite, il y avait le plat principal. Ils ont pu choisir entre les **lasagnes** et le **poulet** à la **moutarde**. Pauline a choisi le poulet mais malheureusement, il était un peu **dur** et il manquait de **sel**. Pour le **dessert**, ils se sont régalés avec un fondant au chocolat délicieux.

QUIZ # 7

a-14.   b-11.   c-13.   d-15.   e-12.   f-6.   g-5.   h-1.   i-16.   j-9.   k-4.   l-7.
m-10.   n-2.   o-8.   p-3.

Voici les directions pour vous rendre au **magasin de vêtements**, depuis la place de la **Fontaine**. Il faut **prendre** la première rue à **droite** et aller jusqu'aux **feux**. Une fois que le feu est vert, tournez à gauche. **Derrière** l'église il y a une station de **métro**. Passez la station et il faudra encore **marcher** pendant 10 minutes. Vous verrez le magasin sur votre gauche.

QUIZ # 8

a-13.   b-6.   c-11.   d-15.   e-12.   f-16.   g-10.   h-14.   i-2.   j-8.   k-4.   l-3.
m-1.   n-5.   o-9.   p-7.

Ma cousine Coline est venue me rendre visite pour mon anniversaire. Son voyage était un vrai cauchemar ! Pour commencer, elle a manqué le **taxi** pour l'amener à l'**aéroport**. Elle a presque raté son **vol**. En descendant de l'avion, elle s'est rendu compte qu'elle avait laissé son **bagage à main** à l'aéroport, qui contenait son portefeuille avec son **passeport** et sa **carte d'identité**. Une fois arrivée en **ville**, il y avait tellement de **touristes** que toutes les rues étaient bloquées par des embouteillages. Elle voulait s'arrêter pour acheter un **gâteau d'anniversaire** mais elle n'a pas pu trouver de boulangerie car elle avait aussi perdu son **guide touristique**. Elle n'avait pas non plus de cadeau, donc elle s'est arrêtée dans le seul magasin ouvert, qui était un magasin de jouets, et elle a acheté un **ours en peluche** vraiment mignon.

Made in the USA
Las Vegas, NV
04 May 2023

71510498R00105